WHAT

WHAT WE HOLD IN TRUST

Rediscovering the Purpose of Catholic Higher Education

Don J. Briel, Kenneth E. Goodpaster
and Michael J. Naughton

FOREWORD BY DENNIS HOLTSCHNEIDER, CM

The Catholic University of America Press
Washington, DC

Library of Congress Cataloging-in-Publication Data

Names: Briel, Don, author. | Goodpaster, Kenneth E., 1944- author.
    | Naughton, Michael, 1960- author. | Holtschneider, Dennis H.,
    1962-writer of foreword.
Title: What we hold in trust : rediscovering the purpose of Catholic higher
    education / Don J. Briel, Kenneth E. Goodpaster and Michael J. Naughton;
    foreword by Dennis Holtschneider.
Description: Washington, DC : The Catholic University of America Press,
    [2021] | Includes bibliographical references and index. | Summary:
    "What We Hold in Trust unfolds in four chapters that will demonstrate
    how essential it is for the faculty, administrators, and trustees of Catholic
    universities to think philosophically and theologically (Chapter One),
    historically (Chapter Two) and institutionally (Chapters Three and
    Four). It concludes with an examination of conscience for university
    leaders and recommended reading. It calls for leaders in Catholic
    universities who understand the roots of the institutions they serve,
    who can wisely order the goods of the university, who know what is
    primary and what is secondary, and who can distinguish fads and
    slogans from authentic reform. These leaders will be in touch with their
    history and have a love for tradition, and in particular for the Catholic
    tradition. Without this vision, our universities may grow in size, but
    shrink in purpose"— Provided by publisher.
Identifiers: LCCN 2021058709 (print) | LCCN 2021058710 (ebook) |
    ISBN 9780813233802 (paperback) | ISBN 9780813233819 (ebook)
Subjects: LCSH: Catholic universities and colleges—United States.
Classification: LCC LC487 .B75 2021 (print) | LCC LC487 (ebook) |
    DDC 378/.0712—dc23
LC record available at https://lccn.loc.gov/2021058709
LC ebook record available at https://lccn.loc.gov/2021058710

TABLE OF CONTENTS

TO DON BRIEL
(1947–2018)

A friend and colleague whose vision, wisdom,

and leadership helped to renew

the Catholic university

FOREWORD

St. Augustine begins his famous *Confessions* with the observation that his early education taught him Greek using stories of heroes and gods who were anything but moral. Authors such as Homer were thrilling but also formative in all the wrong ways. St. Augustine believed he and the young men of his time learned not only the Greek language, but social norms of sexual conquests, political conniving, dissemblance, power grabs, and more from the stories they idealized.

This wasn't an excuse for his early hedonism, nor was it even regretting the life he had led. Augustine's concept of confessing was far larger, marveling at how God acted at every turn to guide him toward something larger and more meaningful. Still, he pondered later in life how that early education shaped his early years and decisions.

Education for wisdom is a suspect proposition in the present age, not least because of our concern over "whose wisdom, exactly?" The promise and potential of a Catholic higher education walks unapologetically into that question with an answer: Jesus Christ.

From Paul to the present day, scholars have probed the more and less satisfactory ways that humanity has named the ineffable ground of our being which we refer to in shorthand with the word, "God." Augustine, and scholars before and since, wondered, too, about the implications of their faith. Was the political arrangement with Rome necessary for the growth of Christianity or was it an unforgiveable moral compromise? Was it moral to enslave other human beings? To enslave people economically with prohibitively onerous loans? To declare war knowing how many innocents would die? To reward human competition but ignore the elderly and developmentally challenged who could not compete? To preserve life on ventilators against a patient or loved one's wishes? To honor national boundaries even when another nation's leadership is slaughtering whole populations within those borders?

Such issues are discussed beyond Christian circles, and yet Christians can hardly pretend that their convictions about God and Jesus Christ do not give them perspective on such matters. Catholics learn to enter a diverse world's conversation using the language of human rights, natural law, literature and art holding to their commitments and able to think aloud with those who name the ineffable in other ways or not at all.

Universities are a subset of this social engagement. A university is a home to educate the next generation in all that has been said before and to encourage its students to knowledgably enter the fray themselves. A place apart to think and wonder about how one's convictions interact with the questions of the day. A place to learn how to achieve a more just and humane world but also to practice respectful disputation, listening to ways in which one might be wrong. Social commitment tempered by humility.

Catholic universities were not founded to convert a world. They were founded to prepare the young for a world desperately in need of principled, caring experts, committed to a view of humanity rising to match what we know of Jesus' own heart, and through him, his Father's. In the process, our universities have welcomed everyone to the table, Catholics and non-Catholics alike—anyone who wants to serve that world together.

Education for wisdom, yes, but so much more. For lives well lived with purpose and meaning. For a social fabric laced with compassion. And so, we require ethics requirements for our students. We require philosophy courses hoping they will find lines of thought that bless a lifetime. We require theology courses that sweep aside romantic notions of God for sometimes unsettling realizations that the Judeo-Christian God means it when he takes the side of the poor. At best, we find the deeply human dimensions of all the subjects we teach.

The authors put forth a particular challenge about how well Catholic universities are doing in sharing this wisdom, this fire. Most of their firepower is focused on administrators, but eventually they tilt their aim toward faculty and trustees. The problem is more than a matter

FOREWORD

of people "who know better but lack the backbone to do it." The problem is that so many administrators, faculty, and trustees do not know the tradition well enough to pass it on. My hope is that this book will reinforce the concerns of those who are already concerned, while motivating those who should be concerned to seek the resources they need to pass on this precious *fire*.

St. Augustine was a man of startling intellectual passions, adopting and rejecting lines of thought with equal verve before settling on one that offered the wisdom and intellectual satisfaction for a life well lived. The breadth of his learning was astounding, as was his ability to draw upon it all as he wrestled with a social fabric that shifted mightily in the dramatic years that were his to lead. In our time, we bring students into that same search, introducing them to the many ideas that shape our world, and daring them to find something ultimately satisfying.

The preparation of the young—and therein the creation of a more just world—is a daunting prospect indeed. Briel, Goodpaster and Naughton deeply love the Catholic intellectual tradition and what it offers the young for a life ahead. They would have us redouble our work to see that it remains vital for future generations. I couldn't agree more. Our students and the world they will lead deserve nothing less.

Rev. Dennis H. Holtschneider, CM
President, Association of Catholic Colleges
and Universities

PREFACE

In 2015, we began writing this essay with the aim of defining more clearly the purpose of the Catholic university and of noting current obstacles to that purpose. We then summarized our thoughts and wrote a short essay in the Jesuit weekly, *America Magazine,* with the intention to finish the larger monograph.[1] In early 2018, Don Briel was diagnosed with two forms of acute leukemia. He was told that his cancer was untreatable and passed away a month later on February 15, 2018. Don's words, voice, and thoughts pervade this work. He played an important formative role in our understanding of Catholic higher education, and we dedicate this text to him.

A father of five children, Don Briel was the founder of the Catholic Studies program, the first of its kind, at the University of St. Thomas (Minnesota) in 1993. He emerged as a leading visionary in Catholic higher education. Steeped in St. John Henry Newman's philosophy of education and possessing a profound grasp of the larger Catholic intellectual tradition, Don was keenly aware of the Catholic university's promise and its challenges, and he had a realistic practical understanding of how the university worked. It was characteristic of his thought that his vision for Catholic higher education was something that could not be simply imposed, but only proposed. He believed that the Catholic university's renewal would be accomplished more by invitation into a positive vision than by policies enforced by decree.

In the final month of his life, many former students came to visit Don, asking one last time for his advice and counsel. It seemed that the approach of death gave Don's always clear mind a yet more luminous quality. Don would tell students that "we have a work that is given to us on which the plan of salvation depends. . . . God could give it to another but in fact this is the deep invitation in each of our lives that we have this great dignity—we're meant for a purpose which we can't fully grasp." This meant that "the main purpose in life is to be attentive. Attentive to the working of grace that invites us to understand that work more deeply and to participate in it more fully."[2]

Don's thought always bore nuance. He recognized that every strength had a corresponding vulnerability. He thus cautioned his students not to let concern about the immediate specifics of their calling obstruct their understanding of life's deeper meaning. He told them that "what God is inviting is a transformation of life and its purpose, not simply a work to be done."

In one of his last interviews, Don Briel commented on his own life's work: "This is not my work, it's not our work, it's God's work, and to have been given this possibility to assist in realizing this great educational vision has been the great privilege of my life."[3] Our hope in publishing this volume is to further that educational vision.[4]

Michael J. Naughton and
Kenneth E. Goodpaster

ENDNOTES

[1] Don Briel, Kenneth Goodpaster and Michael Naughton, "Our Reason for Being: Restoring the Pillars of Catholic Education," *America Magazine,* February 1, 2016. https://www.americamagazine.org/issue/our-reason-being.

[2] Taken from a documentary on Don's life, "*Don Briel: A Life of Purpose and Joy,*" One Billion Stories, 2019, https://www.youtube.com/watch?v=Xz7qiSeElSc.

[3] Maria Wiering. "Ahead of his Feb. 15 death, Catholic Studies founder Don Briel reflected on dying well," *The Catholic Spirit,* February 13, 2018, https://thecatholicspirit.com/news/local-news/told-not-long-live-catholic-studies-founder-don-briel-reflects-dying-well.

[4] We are also grateful to Fr. Dennis Holtschneider, Matt Briel, Fr. Michael Keating, John Martino, and CUAP's referees for their comments on the manuscript. Their insights were invaluable. We also would like to thank our student workers, Rachel Petruconis and Eamon Naughton, for their editorial work.

INTRODUCTION

The Need for Roots

In 1943, the French Jewish philosopher and political activist, Simone Weil, was asked by the French Resistance to prepare a text on the possibilities for rebuilding French society and for effecting a cultural regeneration once the Nazis had been defeated. The essay she wrote was eventually given the title *The Need for Roots.*

According to Weil, having roots was "perhaps the most important and least recognized need of the human soul."[1] Consequently, "[u]prootedness is by far the most dangerous malady to which human societies are exposed."[2] She argued that the sudden collapse of France in June 1940 displayed a kind of "root rot" that was afflicting the country. When a tree falls in a storm, it is often because its roots have been rotting for years under the surface of the soil. Weil held that a spiritual inertia had been plaguing France for many years, with the result that French culture had lost its necessary connection to its past and origins. France thus had little sense of who or what it was, where it was heading, or what was worth fighting for.

For Weil, one poison that tends to destroy the roots of a society is an education that has become disconnected from the deepest dimensions of its culture. Educational practice can wither the roots of a culture when it is dominated by pragmaticism, an agnosticism to the transcendent, a fixation on technical science, and specialization resulting in fragmentation.[3] This kind of education prioritizes the active over the contemplative, the technical over the moral. It erodes the receptive and given nature of the world, creating the illusion that we are, as C. S. Lewis wrote, the "conditioners" or "man moulders" of the world.[4]

Weil's metaphor of roots is an important one for leaders of institutions at this time, especially those of us connected to Catholic universities. We, faculty, administrators and trustees, have been encountering extraordinary headwinds during the last fifty years. Besides a pandemic that has created significant volatility and uncertainty in higher education, universities are facing demographic changes with fewer and more diverse traditional college age students, declining financial margins, cheaper alternative delivery systems as well as high fixed costs of infrastructure and overhead. For many leaders in Catholic universities, economic survival dominates their consciousness.

Great leaders, however, are never concerned only about survival. They know deep in their bones that survival alone makes us little better than brutes. As difficult as bankruptcy can be, leaders of Catholic higher education know that the deeper tragedy is passing on a soulless university that has lost its purpose.

Political scientist Hugh Heclo, in his insightful book *On Thinking Institutionally*, observes that institutions are more than simply tools for accomplishing certain discrete tasks or services.[5] They exist to preserve or advance core principles that we deem "important for their own sake." They are "weathered presences" motivated by our own mortality, structures that have come before us and will succeed us in the pursuit of what we hold dear. The appreciation of this reality, what has been called the "institutional insight," is a critical element of the portfolio of those who would lead Catholic universities into the future.[6]

We are not the creators of the purpose of our universities; we *hold in trust* that purpose as heirs of a two-thousand-year-old educational tradition. This tradition seeks to integrate and express the intellectual, emotional, spiritual, and moral nature of our humanity, often described as "educating the whole person." It is a tradition that fosters "integral human development" through an interdisciplinary approach to education with its deepest roots expressed philosophically and theologically.[7]

Many in leadership roles in Catholic universities today do not come out of these disciplines of theology and philosophy and have had little exposure to them. For this reason, these disciplines can seem foreign, and discussions about their role in the university and especially in the curriculum can be uneasy. Yet leaders—whether faculty, administrators, or trustees—will not be able to understand their role in Catholic universities unless they have a sense of what this tradition means institutionally, and how it shapes the deepest purpose of the university.[8]

Faithfulness to this tradition is not preserving its ashes, but *passing on its fire*.[9] This tradition, often called the Catholic intellectual tradition, has a distinctive purpose for Catholic universities, and it provides the confidence necessary for articulating, cultivating, and making sacrifices for such a purpose, especially in times of crisis. This purpose expresses for the Catholic university its *raison d'être*, the reason for its being, what it is "designed" to do. When leaders are at their best, they create the conditions within their institutions for accomplishing this purpose. They draw upon the university's origins and founding narrative, and tap into the deeper principles that give it meaning and direction. For leaders, institutional purpose serves as a guiding compass that *orders* institutional decision-making in relation to setting strategies, allocating resources, and managing structures and systems.

Unfortunately, we are facing the challenge of living in an institutional world, not of deep roots, but of "cut flowers"— plants with no roots: a world of slogans, branding, and marketing. We often spend more time on branding strategies and marketing plans than on the deep ideas and convictions that underlie a Catholic philosophy of education. While branding and marketing have their place, especially in a digital world, we will find our institutions rapidly losing their vitality if our focus on these activities leads us to lose connection with our roots, and to replace what is primary with what is secondary. We will increasingly default into "strictly instrumental attachments needed to get a particular job done."[10] Cut flowers may look attractive but deprived of the nourishing sources that give them life, they can flourish only for a brief time before they wither and die. Today, as in every age, we as leaders of Catholic universities must heed Simone Weil's counsel: attend to our deepest roots, to the fundamental purpose of the institutions we lead and govern.

Our more specific concern for Catholic universities today comes to this: the Catholic university that sees its *principal* purpose in terms of the active life, of career, and of changing the world, undermines the contemplative and more deep-rooted purpose of the university. If a university adopts the language of technical and social change as its *main* and *exclusive* purpose, it will weaken the deeper roots of the university's liberal arts and Catholic mission. The language of the activist, of changing the world through social justice, equality and inclusion, or of the technician through market-oriented incentives, plays an important role in university life. We need to change the world for the better and universities play an important role, but both the activist and technician will be co-opted by our age of hyper-activity and technocratic organizations if there is not first a contemplative outlook on the world that *receives* reality rather than *constructs* it.[11]

Think about it on a personal level for a moment. If all we do is work and give of ourselves, no matter how noble the cause, we eventually exhaust ourselves. The Latin phrase *nemo dat quod non habet*, "no one gives what he does not have," captures the point. We need to receive what we do not have. If we are to give rightly, we need to learn to receive rightly. We are made not only to work but also to rest, not only to give but also to receive. If we are to get work right, career right, social justice right, we need to get leisure, rest, and receiving right.[12] It takes a long time for many of us to get this. Too often it takes a personal tragedy, a mid-life crisis, or a pandemic to knock us out of the illusion that our identity is only found in our achievements.

For nearly a thousand years, the tradition of the liberal arts situated within Catholic colleges and universities has sought to nurture and protect a *givenness* to reality, a logic of *gift*.[13] The university's purpose as an institution is to encounter the world with wonder and awe, to behold its beauty and receive its goodness and truth. The physical and tangible are a created reality with profound moral and spiritual meaning. This is why the liberal arts entail *both* the sciences and the humanities, not as two compartmentalized kinds of learning but as two ways of human knowledge whereby we can see the whole of reality and not merely its parts.[14] At the heart of the university's life is not only a choice but an encounter, not principally an achievement but a gift. Careers and social concerns are important aspects of a university's life, but by themselves they fail to get to the root of the matter because they can deceive us into thinking that we create ourselves. But when careers and social concerns are rooted in a created reality that is first received in all its wonder and complexity, we are more likely to develop a "disciplined sensitivity" to the whole of life, to a work that goes beyond a mere career, and to a profound awareness of the massive sufferings of humanity.[15] Without such a created reality that fosters a unity of knowledge, universities are prone to reduce their function to career credentialing or purveying ideologies, or even worse, they will do both at the same time.

While every age has its own crisis, our age is distinguished by a culture that has increasingly given up on a created order of the world. And so some have said that our concern in this book is thirty years too late.

The path for most Catholic universities has been set,
we are told, and there is little chance of retrieving any
distinctively contemplative Catholic liberal arts education. Increasingly, utility and action-oriented change in
the form of career credentialing, experiential learning,
health and safety concerns, environmental sustainability and equality policies will be the principal forms used
to express the purpose of the university. These terms
already dominate the language of mission statements,
strategic plans, budget priorities, curriculum reforms,
research agendas and convocation and graduation
speeches. It is argued that if Catholic universities are
to survive in our increasingly pluralistic post-modern
age, they will need to become more secular in terms of
utility and social benefits and less distinctively rooted
in a contemplative vision of life as created.

We believe that this view is short-sighted. A university should be dedicated to knowing what is true
because it is true, not merely because it is useful.
Otherwise, it merely feeds a culture and a politics in
which people make truth claims based largely on
what is useful to them. As important as the active
life is with its pursuit of justice, sustainability, equity,
diversity, inclusivity and careers, it fails to get to the
deepest roots of the university's institutional purpose.
To address this need for roots, our essay will unfold
in four chapters that will demonstrate how essential
it is for the faculty, administrators, and trustees of

our universities to think philosophically and theologically (Chapter One), historically (Chapter Two) and institutionally (Chapters Three and Four). What we desperately need today are leaders in Catholic universities who understand the roots of the institutions they serve, who can wisely order the goods of the university, who know what is primary and what is secondary, and who can distinguish fads and slogans from authentic reform. We need leaders who are in touch with their history and have a love for tradition, and in particular for the Catholic tradition.

Chapter One begins by exploring the two essential intellectual principles upon which all Catholic universities rest—the unity of knowledge and the complementarity of faith and reason. We propose that leaders at Catholic universities need to properly ground the purpose of the university not in an ethic such as diversity or social justice (which are outcomes of a purpose, not the roots of the purpose itself) but rather in the epistemological principles of the unity of knowledge and the complementarity of faith and reason, principles that foster the intellectual virtue of wisdom. We want to be clear that the ethical virtues and principles of social justice, the common good, inclusion as well as addressing issues such as structural injustice, racism, environmental degradation, family breakdown, pornography, secularism, materialism, national and global inequities and other social problems are important realities to the university, but they need a root system that prevents them from ideological disorders if they are to be addressed in a way that is worthy of the university.[16]

Chapter Two explores the historical roots of the university's purpose and where it begins to become disordered. If we are to know who we are and where we are going, we have to know where we have come from. This does not mean slavishly imitating the past, but it does mean that our historical consciousness should enlarge our perspective and free us from naïve self-sufficiency. We should understand that we are part of a tradition, which as G. K. Chesterton once put it, "refuses to submit to the small and arrogant oligarchy of those who merely happen to be walking about. All democrats object to men being disqualified by the accident of birth; tradition objects to their being disqualified by the accident of death."[17] A tradition can protect us from the danger of being mere children of our own age of slogans, brands, and platitudes. It is also our tradition that gives us the ability to see more clearly the problems we face today in higher education.

This historical perspective sets us up to address in Chapter Three a particular leadership problem in Catholic universities we call *teleopathy*. We define teleopathy as a disordering (*pathos*) of goals (*telos*). Teleopathy expresses itself in a three-stage pattern. First, in the absence of a clear understanding of the university's purpose, leaders in Catholic higher education can *fixate* on specialization, careerism or only social and ethical causes as surrogates, which are insufficient to sustain the purpose of a Catholic university. They, then, in the name of pluralism, *rationalize* setting aside a philosophical and theological vision of the university. This ironically leads to less, not more, pluralism, since most other universities propose similar surrogates. Third, they *detach* themselves from the two root principles of the university—the unity of knowledge and the complementarity of faith and reason—leading to a separation of the university from a deeper relationship with the Church and its tradition. This detachment rarely happens all at once, but discrete decisions over many years have the cumulative effect of undermining the purpose of the Catholic university.

In Chapter Four, we propose that faculty, senior leaders, and trustees can avoid this teleopathic pattern by finding ways to "institutionalize" the university's mission – to *pass on the fire* – through identity-enhancing practices such as recruitment and hiring, faculty leadership development, interdisciplinary innovation, and trustee oversight. We then conclude with an "examination of conscience" for educational leaders focusing on the mission and identity of the Catholic university.

The responsibility of leading institutions calls for difficult and complex work and is not for the faint of heart. Unfortunately, our age is increasingly characterized by a narrowing of the purpose of our institutions

to one limited good: in universities to career credentialing; in religion to emotive experience; in business
to shareholder wealth; and in marriage to sentiment
between autonomous individuals. When we "thin out"
institutions this way, flattening them from a vibrant
set of integrated goods to one instrumental or emotive
good, they become ineffective in serving their deep-
rooted purposes.

Many of our institutions have *grown in size*, but
they have *shrunk in purpose*. They may be richer but
not wiser. They have become small spaces, both mor-
ally and spiritually. In a highly individualistic culture
such as ours, we face the challenge to think and act with
what we have referred to as "the institutional insight"
– to pass on institutions as strong and as true to their
purposes as when we were entrusted with them.

At Catholic universities this means we need to
get clear on the fundamental principles that guide
our educational practice, to have a picture of the
overall narrative of Catholic universities, to see disorders that afflict us today, and to find effective ways
to institutionalize our deepest principles. And, above
all, we need to continually examine our consciences,
an examination that will open our minds and hearts
to how the Lord calls us to renew the institutions in
which we live and work.

ENDNOTES

1   Simone Weil, *The Need for Roots: Prelude to a Declaration of Duties towards Mankind* (London: Routledge Classics, 2002), 43. See also Alan Jacobs, *The Year of Our Lord 1943* (New York: Oxford University Press, 2018).

2   Weil, *The Need for Roots,* 47.

3   Weil, *The Need for Roots,* 45. Weil also speaks of money and, in particular, the desire for money as the other poison of cultural roots. The desire for money in universities comes in many forms: among students, a tendency towards careerism that instrumentalizes all learning to career training; among faculty, a tendency towards consumerism that views students as simply customers who are to be satisfied and affirmed rather than challenged and pushed; among administrators, who court outside money from donors with little consideration to the liberal and Catholic nature of the university and focuses instead on rankings and prestige.

4   C. S. Lewis, *The Abolition of Man* (New York: HarperCollins Publishers, 2000), originally published 1944, Chapter Three.

5   Hugh Heclo, *On Thinking Institutionally* (Boulder, Colo.: Paradigm Publishers 2006).

6   Goodpaster, "Human Dignity and the Common Good: The Institutional Insight," *Business and Society Review* 122, no. 1 (March 2017): 35.

7   This theme of integral human development has been a central theme in Catholic social teachings.

8   One of the findings in a study of Catholic university presidents by Melanie Morey and Dennis Holtschneider highlight the "significant lack of formal theological and spiritual preparation among presidents. There is also widespread agreement among presidents that inadequate lay preparation presents a problem for the future of Catholic higher

education. Despite this, few lay presidents (9%) report that they personally feel ill-equipped to lead the religious mission of their institutions." In their study, they found presidents of Catholic universities self-reporting that they felt best prepared "related to the day-to-day operations of their institutions, such as budgeting and financial management, advancement, public relations, admissions, technology, strategic planning, staff development, personnel management, and overall leadership" and a small minority felt "well-prepared to lead the religious mission of their colleges." See Melanie M. Morey and Dennis H. Holtschneider, "Leadership and the Age of the Laity: Emerging Patterns in Catholic Higher Education," in *Catholic Higher Education: An Emerging Paradigm for the Twenty-First Century*, ed. Anthony J. Cernera (Fairfield, Conn.: Sacred Heart University Press, 2005), 13.

9   Variously attributed to Gustav Mahler, St. Thomas More or Sir John Denham. Or, as Plutarch put it, "Education is not the filling of a pail, but the lighting of a fire."

10 Heclo, *On Thinking Institutionally*, 101.

11 Pope Francis states that this contemplative nature "provides the leaven of that universal fraternity which is 'capable of seeing the sacred grandeur of our neighbour, of finding God in every human being, of tolerating the nuisances of life in common by clinging to the love of God." Pope Francis, Apostolic Constitution *Veritatis Gaudium* (January 1, 2018), 4. This educational move away from a contemplative, receptive vision of the world "alters the basic relation of man to reality. He now views reality essentially from a functional point of view. He no longer approaches the world from the viewpoint of contemplation and wonder, but as one who measures, weighs and acts." Joseph

Ratzinger, *Theological Highlights of Vatican II* (New York: Paulist Press, 1966), 162. This new functional account of the human person has increasingly defined the basic philosophy of modern and progressive education and has had unfortunate considerable impact on the vision and educational philosophy of Catholic schools and universities. Christopher Dawson described this problem as the Western mind turning "away from the contemplation of the absolute and eternal to the knowledge of the particular and the contingent. It has made man the measure of all things and has sought to emancipate human life from its dependence on the supernatural. Instead of the whole intellectual and social order being subordinated to spiritual principles, every activity has declared its independence, and we see politics, economics, science and art organizing themselves as autonomous kingdoms which owe no allegiance to any higher power." Christopher Dawson, "Christianity and the New Age," in *Essays in Order* (London: Sheed and Ward, 1931), 66–67.

12   See Michael Naughton, *Getting Work Right: Labor and Leisure in a Fragmented World* (Steubenville, Ohio: Emmaus Road Publishing, 2019).

13   In an insightful essay, Tara Isabella Burton discusses the important philosophical question of "who are we, really": "the idea that there are elements of our humanity—both those within our control and those that come to us as *given,* whether biologically or socially—that are not merely ancillary to who we are but rather at the ontological heart of it. There are elements of our makeup that are not simply qualities we *have*, but constituent parts of what make us *really* us. That we as a society—a philosophically fragmented, quasi-secular (or at least post-Christian) society—have not

negotiated a common understanding of what these realities *are*, and what separates the Real in us from the merely
incidental, does not make the question any less important.
Rather, this uncertainty is at the heart of our politics and our
culture wars alike. A coherent account of who we *are* is the
first step towards a political vision of who we might become."
Tara Isabella Burton, "Nature vs. Nurture: What The Culture
War Is Really About," *The American Interest* (February 10,
2020), https://www.the-american-interest.com/2020/02/10
/what-the-culture-war-is-really-about.

14 Josef Pieper, *Leisure the Basis of Culture* (South Bend, Ind.:
St. Augustine's Press, 1998), see Chapter Two where he
speaks of *ratio* and *intellectus.*

15 Michael Buckley, SJ, *The Catholic University as Promise and
Project* (Washington, D.C.: Georgetown University Press,
1998), 112.

16 Benedict XVI relates the theological idea of charity to justice and the common good and he places charity in truth at
the center of Catholic social teachings rather than justice. He
states, "*Charity goes beyond justice* . . . but it never lacks justice. . . . Justice is the primary way of charity . . . [yet] charity
transcends justice and completes it in the logic of giving and
forgiving." Later he states, "Only in *charity, illumined by the
light of reason and faith,* is it possible to pursue development
goals that possess a more humane and humanizing value."
Benedict XVI, Encyclical Letter *Caritas in veritate* (June 29,
2009), 6–7, 9.

17 G. K. Chesterton, *Orthodoxy* (London: Penguin, 1908), 85.

CHAPTER 1

PURPOSE

*The Two Core Principles of the
Catholic University*

In 1948, Josef Pieper published his book *Leisure:
The Basis of Culture* in Germany. It seemed to be an
utterly irrelevant book for the time, considering that
Germany, a country decimated by the Allies during
World War II, was in need of work, not leisure. Pieper's
post-war publication appeared to be one more book
from one more academic whose isolation in the university's proverbial ivory tower failed to understand
the world he inhabited.

Yet, Pieper anticipated such objections. On the first
page of the book he writes: "To 'build our house' at this
time implies not only securing survival, but also putting
in order again our entire moral and intellectual heri-
tage. And before any detailed plan along these lines can
succeed, our new beginning, our re-foundation, calls
out immediately for ... a defense of leisure."[1] Pieper was

well aware of the Nazi slogan over the gate of Auschwitz
and other concentration camps—"arbeit macht frei"
(work sets you free). Work by itself does not make us
free, but only enslaved to ideology—whether Nazism,
communism, capitalism, careerism, consumerism,
pragmaticism. What makes us free, Pieper argued, is
not work but leisure, and not just any kind of leisure,
but leisure that brings forth an attitude of the mind and
a condition of the soul that fosters a capacity to receive
the reality of the world.

For Pieper, the renewal of culture and in particular of
education calls for a contemplative outlook, the capacity to receive reality rather than only construct it. While
many Catholic colleges and universities are fighting to
survive, the question is "survive to do what?" Certainly
not just to make money or pass on career credentials
or the ideology of the day. As noted by others, persons
who marry the spirit of this age will find themselves
widowers in the next. The Catholic university's educational project as it developed out of the long Western
tradition, discussed in the next chapter, is to pass on
this contemplative outlook in terms of two intellectual
principles that give it its distinctive character.

(1)   The Principle of the **Unity of Knowledge:** Because
      the world is a cosmos created by a God of order,
      there is a coherence to all that exists, and a result-
      ing correspondence between the order of reality

and the human enterprise of gaining knowledge. An essential grasp of the whole is necessary for an understanding of its constituent parts. Thus, individual disciplines designed to investigate one facet of that whole need to be pursued within an interdisciplinary context of mutual relations, thereby clarifying both the strengths and limits of each particular field of study.

(2) The Principle of the **Complementarity of Faith and Reason:** Grasping the entirety of truth demands different modes of understanding and investigation. Truths arrived at through reason and truths understood through Revelation are each rooted in a common source, the God who is Truth, and are therefore ultimately complementary to one another.

Fostering a commitment to these intellectual principles clarifies the purpose of the university as an *institution* and helps to make clear the mission and identity of Catholic higher education. Understanding these principles and their implications for today's world is critical for all leaders in Catholic universities. Unfortunately, neither of these principles is easily comprehended by our current secular and increasingly technocratic culture. As Pope Francis stated at a conference with educators, "For me, the greatest crisis of education, . . . is being closed to transcendence."[2] Our hope in this chapter is to help leaders in Catholic higher education to see the value of these principles for an educational vision that can guide them in their day-to-day decisions. This is especially true for a society that is increasingly diverse and pluralistic. For pluralism to flourish, we have to speak from our *center*—not from our boundaries or peripheries—but we must do so in a way that invites others to do the same. Peripheries are safe and comfortable, but ultimately dissatisfying, creating flat and mediocre lives, landing us in the shallows of the "least common denominator," places that lack the potency to form community and build the common good. When we speak from our center we begin to get at the deeper roots and what we find to be ultimately true. These deeper realities can never be *imposed* but only *proposed*. But we are facing, as we will discuss below, a generation of students that is increasingly unsure about *what its center is.* A Catholic liberal education should help students think in terms of first principles, of deep roots, of centers, but the university itself needs to know what its own principles are.

1. THE UNITY OF KNOWLEDGE

What is it that makes a Catholic university education "universal"? A first answer to that question is that a university investigates everything; no field of study is neglected in its curriculum. But there is a second important aspect of "universal" that has gotten almost entirely lost: the university also seeks to *integrate* all knowledge, including religious knowledge, within a coherent universal account of reality.

Albert Einstein once said, "the most incomprehensible thing about the universe is that it is comprehensible."[3] This comprehensibility is at the heart of what makes a *uni*versity a place where the *unity* of knowledge can be discovered. As our colleague John Boyle says: "Everything from God to dirt is ordered and related to each other in significant and intelligible ways." The brilliant young Indian Hindu mathematician, Srinivasa Ramanujan (1887–1920), wrote that "an equation for me has no meaning unless it expresses a thought of God."[4] Mathematics for him was part of a larger created order. He saw patterns in everything from the color in light to reflections in water—all of which could be mathematized, revealing themselves in the most intricate patterns and reflecting a created cosmos. Ramanujan and his way of reasoning have much to teach Catholic universities. He embraced a contemplative outlook that listened "to the being of things,"[5] that worked through wonder, imagination, and intuition. He was thus able to see order and unity through mathematical patterns where other people saw only randomness and chaos.

Education is an introduction to reality, to a cosmos not only of immense complexity but also one of extraordinary unity.[6] No single academic discipline can independently provide an accurate account of the whole; it requires many disciplines to begin to understand the totality of reality. A proper interdisciplinary engagement by the university thus provides a unique forum by which each discipline is informed, checked, balanced, corrected, complemented, and completed by the contributions of all the others. John Henry Newman insisted that a person trained narrowly in one field was not competent even in his chosen area, for he could not see where his or her specialized knowledge applied and where it did not.[7]

Thus an economic account of human life needs to be supplemented by and integrated with an historical account, with sociological and psychological accounts, and with philosophical and theological accounts. There is a temptation in each discipline to monopolize knowledge and to explain everything in life through its methods and insights—a kind of greedy reductionism. So if the study of economics, say, is cut off from political science, or ethics, or law, or perhaps especially from theology, that study will not be merely incomplete, but fundamentally disordered. Many people have noted that Oscar Wilde's famous quip concerning the cynic can be applied equally well to the economist who may know the price of everything but the value of nothing. This reductionism creates not wisdom but foolishness.[8]

Nonetheless, the claim that there is a unity of knowledge is highly contentious. The objection that

gets raised is not simply due to alternative and conflict-
ing accounts of the nature of that unity, such as Christianity, Confucianism, Kantianism, and so on. It comes
from a different *kind* of claim. Alasdair MacIntyre has
described this counterclaim:

> [that there is] no such thing as the order of things of
> which there could be a unified, if complex, under-
> standing or even a movement toward such an
> understanding. There is on this contemporary view
> nothing to understanding except what is supplied by
> the specialized and professionalized disciplines and
> subdisciplines and subsubdisciplines.[9]

This kind of chaotic intellectual environment in which
the student goes from one department to the next,
bouncing back and forth between various disciplines
and specialties that have no connection or even conversation with each other, not only fragments *knowledge;* it also fragments *students.* How we integrate or fail
to integrate our knowledge will have a lot to do with
whether *we* are integrated or fragmented people.

When the principle of the unity of knowledge is
abandoned, universities tend to turn to "critical thinking" as the principal habit of mind they try to inculcate.
If thinking critically means learning to distinguish the
true from the false, the genuine from the inauthentic,
and the rational from the illogical, it has always been

an important aspect of a well-trained mind, and its promotion has been a signal contribution by the university to the wider society. But if critical thinking is not
to result in a corrosive habit of mind that dissolves all
certitudes and ends in destroying the process of thinking itself, it needs to be founded on a positive understanding of the cosmos, one that is given by the Creator.
When we tell our students to "think for themselves," to
"question authority," to "overcome tradition," to "sub-
vert establishments," without a confidence that there
is an order, a *creation* not of their making, an attitude
that Newman called "creative thinking," students not
only think *for* themselves, but they eventually think
only *of* themselves. When universities introduce students to "critical views" without first introducing them
to a created and objective order, they tend to produce
skepticism not only of authority, tradition, history, and
religion, but also of reality itself, resulting in a paralysis
of self-doubt.

This is a serious challenge for the current generation
of students often called the iGen or Gen Z.[10] Like every
generation, they come to the university with their own
gifts and challenges. A particular challenge for them is
a disproportionately higher rate of depression, psychological distress, and suicidal thoughts and actions than
what previous generations have encountered. While
iGeners are increasingly connected technologically and
are more tolerant and less rebellious than generations

before them, they are also more emotionally fragile. We constantly tell them that they are free to be whoever they want to be, that they should believe in themselves, and that they should follow their own dreams. But such freedoms seemingly make them anxious and unhappy rather than liberated and fulfilled. Popular culture has fed them a continuous diet of self-creationism, according to which they are free to create their own identity and their own world, a world and an identity where nothing is given, and all is constructed. But this leap into "freedom" imparts to students not confidence, but self-doubt, unease, loneliness, and victimhood.

Among the many issues facing our university students and their educational institutions, one of particular importance has to do with the meaning of freedom in its relationship to the unity of truth. In the Catholic and classical tradition, the liberal arts were called "liberal" because they were seen to bring their possessors freedom; freedom *from* ignorance, from irrationality, from uncontrolled desires, and from bias and prejudice, such that the mind and the spirit could be free *to* pursue an objectively true reality. The contemporary view of freedom is entirely different and greatly reduced. We consider ourselves free when we have maximized our ability to choose whatever we wish at any given moment. Yet, "freedom to choose" often leads to the very opposite of freedom. Having a choice between a hundred different cereal brands every day does not make us free, especially if our choices lead to obesity.[11] Instead, freedom is to be found in the ordering of our choices toward what is genuinely excellent and what will make us excellent. It involves more than the ability to choose this or that; it touches on the objective goodness of the choice itself. Servais Pinckaers, OP, describes these two ideas of freedom as the freedom *of indifference* versus the freedom *for excellence*.[12] How we understand freedom determines whether we flourish or become enslaved, whether we serve the good with excellence or grow indifferent to it.

Simply put, our freedom of indifference is only a so-called freedom that pays no attention to any sense of unity: not to a common human nature, nor a common good, nor one God. Its focus is the will of the individual. It involves being free from religion, parents, and institutions, from any normative view of the world and any notion of truth, such that each individual can choose what each wants within a minimal set of limits. When exercising freedom of indifference, the highest value is not the content of the choice, but the fact of the choice itself.

On the other hand, freedom for excellence is based on the idea that we are made *for* something—that we *need* certain things for our true fulfillment. This notion of excellence does not come simply from the willfulness of the individual, but from how this will responds to a larger created order. Excellence comes from the Greek word *arête* which means strength or virtue, namely those internal qualities that allow one to fulfill the purpose of something. For example, anyone has the choice to bang on a piano, but this simply makes noise not music. As George Weigel explains, "learning to play the piano is a matter of some drudgery as we toil over exercises that seem like a constraint, a burden. But as our mastery grows, we discover a new, richer dimension of freedom: we can play the music we like, we can even create music on our own. Freedom, in other words, is a matter of gradually acquiring the capacity to choose the good and to do what we choose with perfection."[13] Again, our freedom operates not out of a chaos of arbitrary wills, but from a deep sense of an order to things. Pinckaers explains that the freedom for excellence "requires the slow, patient work of moral education in order to develop."[14] Such an order is difficult at times to discern, but in such freedom of discernment we commit to authentic and binding relationships that provide the context for developing our internal capacities as human beings. Freedom for excellence, arising from a created order, informs our lives' meaning and undergirds our committed relationships with others. Freedom of indifference, cut off from the cosmos, lands us in an isolated world of loneliness and meaninglessness.

John Paul II, in his letter to Catholic universities, connects this desire for excellence and its unity with the thirst for truth. He argued that the university must go beyond the specialized focus of individual disciplines and "work towards a higher synthesis of knowledge, in which alone lies the possibility of satisfying that thirst for truth which is profoundly inscribed on the heart of the human person."[15] In order to accomplish this synthesis, he thought it would be necessary to develop "interdisciplinary studies, assisted by a careful and thorough study of philosophy and theology" in order to "enable students to acquire an organic vision of reality and to develop a continuing desire for intellectual progress."[16]

The pursuit of truth within this interdisciplinary perspective creates what Newman, in his *Idea of a University,* called the "circle of knowledge." This circle illustrates the conditions needed to develop the "philosophical habit of mind," to see things in relation to one another so as to make good judgments about reality. That habit involves "the power of viewing many things at once as one whole, of referring them severally to their true place in the universal system, of understanding their respective values, and determining their mutual dependence." It gives to its possessors "the clear, calm, accurate vision and comprehension of all things, as far as the finite mind can embrace them, each in its place, and with its own characteristics upon it." Under this habit of mind "the elements of the physical and moral world, sciences, arts, pursuits, ranks, offices, events, opinions, individualities, are all viewed as one, with correlative functions, and as gradually by successive combinations converging, one and all, to the true center." A mind rightly cultivated in this manner "is almost prophetic from its knowledge of history; it is almost heart-searching from its knowledge of human nature; it has almost supernatural charity from its freedom from littleness and prejudice; it has almost the repose of faith, because nothing can startle it; it has almost the beauty and harmony of heavenly contemplation, so intimate is it with the eternal order of things and the music of the spheres."[17]

Within the circle of knowledge that collectively covers the whole of reality, two areas of study, theology and philosophy, are to be given a certain privileged role in ordering the other disciplines due to the foundational and synthetic quality of their subject matter. Theology, or faith seeking understanding, investigates and reflects on the truths of Revelation and brings those supernatural truths to bear on all aspects of knowledge. We will address this in more detail in the next section. Philosophy, seeking the integration of natural reason in all its forms, complements the insights of theology and assists in perceiving its larger implications. When theology and philosophy are marginalized within the university, the result is not merely a vacuum but rather a disordering of the relations of all the other disciplines which then inevitably overstep their competences by moving in to fill the missing elements.[18]

One particular way this disorder manifests is described in philosophy and the social sciences as the

Circle of Knowledge

total separation of "is" from "ought" or of "facts" from "values." This dichotomy is often associated with economic and legal positivism, in which "facts" are viewed as empirically verifiable and capable of truth or falsity, while "values" are seen as matters of subjective preference—and therefore not capable of truth or falsity. Normative claims of right and wrong, good and bad, virtue and vice, are, on this view, relegated to a realm of emotion rather than reason. This perspective not only runs counter to the Greek, Roman, and Judeo-Christian roots of Western thought expressed in the tradition of the liberal arts of history, science, literature, fine arts, mathematics, philosophy, and theology; it also puts into question the ability to make any kind of non-subjective moral claim whatsoever. Can we really accept that it is a purely subjective matter that murder and human trafficking are wrong, that kindness is better than cruelty, that an honest life is better than a dishonest life? Oxford philosopher Mary Midgley explains the vital, productive role of moral judgment:

> The power of moral judgement is, in fact, *not* a luxury, *not* a perverse indulgence of the self-righteous. *It is a necessity*. When we judge something to be bad or good, better or worse than something else, we are taking it as an example to aim at or avoid. Without opinions of this sort, we would have no framework of comparison for our own policy, no chance of profiting by other people's insights or mistakes. In this vacuum, we could form no judgments on *our own* actions.[19]

A curricular manifestation in many colleges and universities of the marginalizing of the humanities by the social and natural sciences (the marginalizing of "values" from "facts") is the separation of moral education from professional education in business, engineering, law, and medicine. The separation of theological and philosophical discourse from these professional disciplines prevents professionals from fully comprehending and taking responsibility for their moral agency. In the context of business administration, for example, it is clear that topical scandals boost the attention given to "business ethics" (e.g., Enron, the subprime mortgage crisis), but it is just as clear that a single mandatory course in professional ethics is insufficient to institutionalize or enculturate a mindset committed to conscience in corporate decision making.

This also brings into focus the "serious error of our age" that the Second Vatican Council called the divided life, and the difficulty of the modern person to confront his or her own inherent division. We can hope that in Catholic colleges and universities, both the marginalization of the normative disciplines in the humanities and their separation from professional education can be thoroughly avoided as a matter of mission, and that the *integration*, not the *fragmentation*, of knowledge can be a distinguishing mark.

We should add that one of the most serious dangers of minimizing the importance of the normative disciplines of philosophy and theology in the humanities is that normative judgments do *not* disappear in favor of so-called "factual" judgments. Instead, they reappear in an *undisciplined* and *unaccountable* fashion within the "value free" spaces of the social and natural sciences, as well as in the policy making of administrators.

Academics and administrators abhor a normative vacuum, even one that they themselves have helped to create in curricular reform projects. The reality is that normativity will reassert itself in an *underground* way once it has been depleted or banished *ex officio*! Unfortunately, when normativity rises from the underground, it is not subject to the disciplines of reason or revelation, it is simply the product of prejudice or the cultural pressures of the day. This affects freedom of speech on campuses, invitations of outside speakers, freedom of assembly, access to student media platforms. Even entire administrative offices are devoted to "enforcing" some of these "undisciplined" norms.

There is a natural rhythm of empirical research and normative affirmation in the university curriculum. Untethered prescriptions or imperatives based on insufficient evidence or outright prejudice need to be held to account philosophically and theologically if the Catholic university is to maintain its perennial identity. If the normative disciplines of philosophy and theology begin to lose their influence and centrality in the curriculum, the "sciences" (and especially the "social" sciences) are in danger of filling the scholarly normative vacuum with unscholarly normative prescriptions. That is, norms will emerge in a university context either responsibly or irresponsibly, either with accountability or with no accountability. We see evidence of the latter in the emergence of "political correctness" and the imposition of speech codes on university campuses. Political action, often in the name of "social justice," serves as a surrogate or substitute for deliberate thoughtful philosophical and theological debate. Administrative fiat begins to take the place of scholarly reason, because the disciplines that act as curricular guardians of reason have been practically weakened if not banished.

2. THE COMPLEMENTARITY OF FAITH AND REASON

The principle of the unity of knowledge must be joined by a second principle: the complementarity of faith and reason. The Catholic university has been given the responsibility and the opportunity to bring together in confident dialogue these two modes of gaining knowledge: on the one hand the open-ended search for all the truths available to human reason, and on the other the grasp and investigation of all the truths that have been made known through the fount of truth, the *Logos,* Jesus Christ.[20] In the context of this dialogue, each participant gains from the other. Without the dialogue, faith is often reduced to a mere emotive principle of private taste rather than a divine gift, and reason reduced to a mechanical pursuit of empirical results that suffocates meaning.

One of the extraordinary claims of Christianity is that Jesus is the *Logos.* We translate *Logos* as Word, but in Greek it also means "reason."[21] *Logos* for the Greeks was a power of the mind that enables us to see a created order imprinted upon the universe. This *logos,* this power, is used to describe many of our disciplines: bio*logy*, geo*logy*, socio*logy*, psycho*logy*, anthropo*logy*. These are human disciplines, forms of reason, of *logos,* that help us to see patterns of how the world works. At a Catholic university, the *Logos,* the Divine, Creative Reason, is connected to and in dialogue with the reason found in these disciplines as well as in literature, mathematics, philosophy, physics, politics, history, economics, the fine arts, and the professions. As the Second Vatican Council explains, "It is only in the mystery of the Word made flesh that the mystery of man truly becomes clear."[22] A Catholic university is a place of interdisciplinary engagement between faith—the Divine *Logos*—and human reason that opens up and explores this wonder and mystery of our existence in all its ramifications.[23] The dialogue between faith and reason supports and sustains the *unity of knowledge*, and resists the forces of specialization that lead to disciplinary isolation and fragmentation.[24] Christ as *Logos,* as Creative Reason, is the root of the contemplative outlook that gives us the power to listen to the being of things, a power that moves us to an imagination, not of make believe, but a way of seeing that within the physical order there operates a spiritual and moral order.[25]

Such an education cultivates the intellect by developing habits of mind to see things in relation to one another, leading to true and accurate judgments about the world.

The Catholic faith and its intellectual tradition, developed over thousands of years, bring to the university a language of deep interiority and ultimate finality that elevate and expand the mind. The doctrines and insights concerning such matters as grace, sin, freedom, redemption, incarnation, and God bring a depth to the university's task of inquiry, and inspire patterns of virtue and sacrifice that can order the university's common life.[26] Faith brings to the university a formation of the soul that addresses aspects of life important for every young person, such as the search for meaning, a logic of gift, the need for a rich inner life that confronts one's nobility and failings, the discernment of one's vocation in work and marriage, one's contribution to the common good, and the forging of bonds of friendship that go beyond mere utility and pleasure.

Cultural commentator and columnist David Brooks highlights the importance of investigations opened up by faith commitments, and the cost when the language and concepts of faith are set aside. Speaking of such investigations, he notes that:

> the religious theologians have been doing it well for a long time. And they just have a better vocabulary for it. So, whether it's Rabbi Soloveitchik or Augustine or

Dorothy Day, they're used to it. They have a language for it and they have a structure for it. They have concepts like sin; they have concepts like virtue, redemption, forgiveness. They have concepts like grace, which is being open and receptive to the unmerited love of God. They have a lot of concepts. And it's like trying to do physics without concepts like gravity, neutron. You really can't do it without the concepts.[27]

Brooks's concern points to the tendency of certain disciplines to want to monopolize knowledge and marginalize the humanities, especially theology. While business, engineering, and the sciences are of undeniable importance, they can take students only so far down the road to understanding the totality of reality and its meaning. Without a comprehensive intellectual tradition within which they can be situated, professional and scientific disciplines come to believe that they can explain everything. As a result, they often foster careerist, materialistic, and consumeristic views of the world that attack the receptive nature of the university.

According to the Catholic intellectual tradition, faith enhances reason, and far from replacing it, faith ennobles reason. In the well-known phrase of Thomas Aquinas, grace perfects nature without destroying or removing it. Faith prevents reason from being reduced to its instrumental tendencies; it connects reason to metaphysical questions, questions of value, purpose, meaning, and ultimacy. Through the encounter with the living God who is truth, faith opens up "new horizons extending beyond the sphere of reason. [It is] a purifying force for reason itself. From a theological standpoint, faith liberates reason from its blind spots and therefore helps it to do its work more effectively and to see its proper object more clearly."[28] While reason retains its own integrity and its proper finality and autonomy, faith contributes to its work by locating the objects of reason's own inquiry, in matters such as science, business, and literature, on "the widest possible conceptual map."[29]

On the other hand, "religion always needs to be purified by reason in order to show its authentically human face."[30] When faith becomes disconnected from reason, especially at the level of academic discourse, and places itself on the margins of human culture, the scope of faith is reduced "at an enormous price to human development."[31] Reason enriches faith by protecting it from the vices of fideism, sentimentality, and superstition. These tendencies are especially present in a highly secular society, where those who profess faith are prone to defensive reactions tending to sectarianism and fundamentalism. In one way or another, such expressions privatize faith and either restrict its animating influence to personal matters alone or create enclaves of life and thought that attempt to escape from the demands of the wider world through tribalism, popularism, or parochialism.

When the truths gained through Revelation seem to contradict truths arrived at using natural reason, the contradiction is only apparent. In such cases there is either a misunderstanding concerning the meaning of Revelation, or an error in the process of natural reasoning. A Catholic university brings a bracing courage to its pursuit of the truth with the conviction that no genuine truth need be feared. Such an approach to the intellectual project is what made possible that *gaudium de veritate* (joy in the truth) that St. Augustine once praised as the realization of the dignity of human thought, and that has characterized the Church's intellectual life through the centuries.[32]

The relationship between faith and reason in the modern university has not been stress-free. It is true that some in the sciences and social sciences have been hostile to theology and to the humanities in general. They have actively sought to exclude all reference to faith, seeking instead to explain all of life through scientific method and instrumental rationality. But the principal problem is elsewhere: it arises from a disordered theology. James Burtchaell has noted that the estrangement of faith from academic life "was not so much the work of godless intellectuals as of pious educators who, since the onset of pietism, had seen religion as embodied so uniquely in the personal profession of faith that it could not be seen to have a stake in social learning."[33] Such pietists lacked confidence in

the ability of faith to engage reason and thereby produce deeper judgments concerning the various disciplines within the university and a more integrated
understanding of the whole.

A contemporary expression of this type of pietism
can be seen in a new "spiritual approach" embraced by
some Catholic universities as they invite greater inclusion and diversity by suppressing the doctrinal claims
of Catholicism for the universally and generically spiritual.[34] The hope of this new approach, one that might
loosely be characterized by the typical contemporary
sentiment, "I am spiritual but not religious," is to find a
way to hold on to some semblance of the spiritual life by
making the contours of spirituality as open and vague
as possible. The thought is that if we drop the doctrines,
duties, laws, and any intellectual claims of faith, what
remains will be a non-divisive spirituality open to all,
expressed largely in terms of searching without landing. The problem with this approach is that first, like
pietism in general, it guts spiritual questions of any
intellectual seriousness, and that second, it does not
work even as spirituality.

While there is an important role for spiritual ecu-
menism where different faith traditions share what they
have in common, the separation between religion and
spirituality endangers both religion and spirituality.
Many boomers, Gen Xers, and millennials (those generations that were beneficiaries of a religious tradition

which passed on the spiritual fruits of the faith) have dropped religion but still hold on to spirituality. The next generation, the iGeners, more and more do not believe in God or the afterlife, don't pray, and simply don't identify as "spiritual."[35] The reasons for these trends are complex—such as the technocratic culture of young people absorbed in their screens and eschewing face to face encounters. The iGen has had little exposure to religion (or in some cases only exposure to unreasonable or politicized versions of it), which has led to a marginalization not only of religion, but also of spirituality, mystery, wonder, and awe. What is becoming evident is that a non-doctrinal, vaguely spiritual approach to life does not have the sustaining power needed in an increasingly secular and technological age.

Glenn Tinder, in an insightful essay entitled "Can We Be Good Without God?" asks:[36] "Can we affirm the dignity and equality of individual persons—values we ordinarily regard as secular—without giving them transcendental backing?" And then he asks further: "To what extent are we now living on moral savings accumulated over many centuries but no longer being replenished? To what extent are those savings already severely depleted?" The implications of Tinder's questions, and his carefully argued negative answers to them, should give us pause about the *sustainability* of the outlook of those who would be "spiritual but not religious."

The separation of faith from reason leaves both impoverished, but it is especially disastrous for the proper exercise of reason. When the transcendent purpose found in Revelation is no longer viewed as knowledge, the world of practical and instrumental reason becomes immune from moral and spiritual critique, leading to many unfortunate consequences in the wider society. As the knowledge that comes through faith has been abandoned among us, the very centers of reasoned thought—our universities—have begun to lose their confidence in reason. This counterintuitive development and dangerous situation point to an important task for Catholic universities. In an astute comment during a lecture with university presidents and faculty in 1998, Cardinal Francis George argued that a university without an integrating vision, a vision that might bring into ordered relation the unity of knowledge and the complementarity of faith and reason, was merely a high-class trade school.[37] Such an institution might produce well-trained technicians, but it could not inspire that wonder and awe, that search for the noble and the true, that serves as the basis of civilization, of a good society, and of human flourishing. The Catholic university, with the spiritual and intellectual resources of the Catholic faith available to it, is thus uniquely positioned to assist in the necessary renewal of the dialogue between faith and reason.[38]

CONCLUSION

The two guiding principles of Catholic higher education, the unity of knowledge and the complementarity
of faith and reason, result in the acquisition of *wisdom*.
They foster wisdom by *receiving* reality rather than *con-
structing* it. Yet wisdom seems increasingly elusive in
our universities. In the words of T. S. Eliot: "Where is
the wisdom we have lost in knowledge? Where is the
knowledge we have lost in information?"[39] We are
flooded with information and knowledge, but we are
starving for wisdom.[40]

This starvation diet is seen most clearly in the
context of the kind of professional education that
increasingly dominates the landscape of most modern universities. We starve our students of wisdom
when we train graduates to be careerists and specialists in their fields alone (information and knowledge
without wisdom), and when we educate them to think
instrumentally with no philosophical or theological
root system. The result of such narrow training creates
specialists without spirit, politicians without heart,
and businesspeople without principle.[41]

Among the more important contributions of
universities is the formation of wise leaders for the
professions. Robert Coles, the famous child psychi-
atrist who taught for many years at Harvard Medical
School, quipped that it is possible to get "all A's and

flunk ordinary living."[42] He had his medical students read the *Diary of a Country Priest* by George Bernanos because it challenged them to see medicine as the treatment of whole persons, not simply individual diseases. Literature that plums the theological depth of the person can educate future doctors to develop a deep instinct, an imaginative vision, to see not only the visible disease but also the dignified person made in the image of God destined for eternal life whose disease is being addressed. As with all professions, medicine needs an inherent moral and spiritual quality in its practice.

This is why Newman established in his Dublin university a school of commerce, a school of law, and a school of medicine. He believed that the integrity of those schools depended upon the overall context of the university; without that context professional schools would simply train students in technical skills. Because of the increasing power of technology and science, integrating and connecting liberal education and professional education, and engaging all the disciplines in a dialogue with the knowledge that comes from faith, has never been more important.

How did we come to this point? If our universities were founded by visionaries like the great religious orders as well as by great minds such as Newman who understood the unity of knowledge and the complementarity of faith and reason, why are these principles increasingly marginal to our institutions? It is to history that we now turn, before we offer our own diagnosis and prognosis for the renewal of Catholic institutions.

ENDNOTES

1   Josef Pieper, *Leisure: The Basis of Culture* (South Bend, Ind.: St. Augustine's Press, 1998), 3. Pieper goes on to make the connection between leisure and education by noting the etymological roots: "The Greek word for leisure (σχολή) is the origin of Latin *scola*, German *Schule*, English *school*. The names for the institutions of education and learning mean 'leisure'" (3–4).

2   Pope Francis "Pope's Q-and-A on the Challenges of Education," *Zenit,* (November 23, 2015), https://zenit.org /articles/pope-s-q-and-a-on-the-challenges-of-education. When education, and especially university education, loses a sense of transcendence, it becomes even more prone to one of the most dangerous vices of the university—intellectual pride. This pride, and the achievements often associated with it, create in academics a certain *bent* in upon themselves (*incurvatus in se,* curved in around oneself). Bishop Robert Barron explains that this pride, this bent into ourselves "is the reduction of reality to the infinitely small space of the ego's concerns and preoccupations." What is needed is a transcendent breaking through "of the buffered and claustrophobic self" to foster "the activity of the *magna anima* (the great soul)." To see the

intellectual pride on display in academics as well as those in the church see Chapter 5 of C.S. Lewis's *The Great Divorce* (New York: Macmillan Publishing Company, 1946). See Bishop Robert Barron, "A Bishop Explains Why You Should Read C.S. Lewis' Masterpiece *The Great Divorce*," https://www.ewtn.com/catholicism/library/bishop -explains-why-you-should-read-cs-lewis-masterpiece -the-great-divorce-3032.

3   Albert Einstein, "Physics and Reality," *Journal of the Franklin Institute* 221, no. 3 (March 1936): 349–382.

4   Srinivasa Ramanujan, statement to a friend, quoted in Shiyali Ramamrita Ranganathan, *Ramanujan: the Man and the Mathematician* (Seoul: Asian Publishing House, 1967), 88. See also the film *The Man Who Knew Infinity* (2015) that describes his life and the deeply spiritual character of his mind.

5   Pieper, *Leisure: The Basis of Culture,* 11.

6   Luigi Giussani, *The Risk of Education,* trans. Mariangela Sullivan (Montreal: McGill-Queen's University Press, 2019), 25ff.

7   John Henry Newman, *The Idea of a University* (Notre Dame, Ind.: University of Notre Dame Press, 1987), 131.

8   As MacIntyre more amusingly put it: "We always need to remind ourselves of something that experience on university committees irritatingly often confirms, that it is possible to have become a highly distinguished historian, say, or physicist and yet remain a fool." Alasdair MacIntyre, "Catholic Universities: Dangers, Hopes, Choices," in *Higher Learning and Catholic Traditions,* ed. Robert E. Sullivan (Notre Dame, Ind.: University of Notre Dame Press, 2001), 3.

9   MacIntyre, "Catholic Universities: Dangers, Hopes, Choices," 6–7.

10   One researcher addressing our current generation is Jean
      Twenge, a psychologist from San Diego State University. She
      concludes that the reason for the decline in mental health
      noted above is related to how young people spend their lei-
      sure, especially in front of a screen. Here is what she says:
      "I didn't come to that conclusion [about leisure] immedi-
      ately or lightly. I came to that conclusion because nothing
      else fits. . . . In some ways it was a process of elimination.
      If you consider what affected 12- to 25-years-olds most in
      2017 versus 2008, one of the biggest differences is the shift
      in how young people spend their *leisure time.* ... They
      spend less time sleeping, less time with friends face-to-
      face, and more time with digital media" (see Jean Twenge,
      "Have Smart Phones Destroyed a Generation," https://www
      .theatlantic.com/magazine/archive/2017/09/has-the
      -smartphone-destroyed-a-generation/534198). Leisure is
      no longer something that refreshes, reorders, or reorients
      students. The significant increase in screen time and less face-
      to-face engagement has left this generation with less commu-
      nity and more loneliness, anxiety, angst, and unease. It is what
      Thomas Aquinas and the moral tradition of the Church called
      in Latin *acedia*, or what we translate as sloth, one of the seven
      deadly sins. Sloth for Aquinas and the tradition is not simply
      a physical laziness but principally a spiritual one. *Acedia* is a
      restlessness of spirit that creates a "despairing refusal to be
      oneself" precisely because the self does not receive, contem-
      plate, and truly rest (see Pieper, *Leisure: The Basis of Culture*,
      28). Pieper is quoting philosopher Søren Kierkegaard.

11   See Barry Schwartz' popular TED talk, "Our Loss of Wisdom,"
      (https://ed.ted.com/lessons/our-loss-of-wisdom-barry
      -schwartz) as well as Barry Schwartz, *The Paradox of Choice:
      Why More is Less* (New York: Ecco, 2004).

12   Servais Pinckaers, OP, *Sources of Christian Ethics* (Washington, D.C.: The Catholic University of America Press, 1995), 354–378.

13   George Weigel, "A Better Concept of Freedom," *First Things* (March 2002), http://www.firstthings.com/article/2002/03/a-better-concept-of-freedom.

14   Pinckaers, *Sources of Christian Ethics,* 359.

15   John Paul II, *Ex corde ecclesiae* (1990), 15. http://www.vatican.va/content/john-paul-ii/en/apost_constitutions/documents/hf_jp-ii_apc _15081990_ex-corde-ecclesiae.html.

16   John Paul II, *Ex corde ecclesiae,* 16. http://www.vatican.va/content/john-paul-ii/en/apost_constitutions/documents/hf_jp-ii_apc_15081990_ex-corde-ecclesiae.html. What an education should do for young people is introduce them to reality, not in any imposing way, but in what Luigi Giussani calls a tradition that serves as an "explanatory hypothesis of reality." He explains that "[n]o discovery can be made- that is, no new step may be taken, no contact with reality may be generated by the person- except through a set idea of the possible meanings. This idea, whether more or less explicit, is nonetheless present and active. Fundamentally the working hypothesis gives people certainty about the positivity of their endeavors, without which nothing happens and nothing is achieved." Giussani, *The Risk of Education,* 28.

17   Newman, *The Idea of a University*, Discourse Six, section 6.

18   The alienation of empirical studies from normative understanding in theology and philosophy is a case in point. Arguing from observations about current social preferences or demographics to claims about *justice*, for example, calls for a move from "is" to "ought" that is seldom

PURPOSE 49

examined rigorously. And if justice is treated carelessly in the social arena, how much higher is the risk that it will be treated carelessly in matters of the human heart. Theology and philosophy are the disciplines that attend not only to the unity of knowledge in the macrocosm, but also to the appropriation of that knowledge in the human soul. The terrible irony is that in too many Catholic universities, required theological and philosophical studies are on the decline, although for some it is self-inflicted because of their own incoherence.

19 Emphasis added. Mary Midgley, "On Trying Out One's New Sword," in *Heart and Mind: The Varieties of Moral Experience*, (New York: St. Martin's Press,1981), 72. Midgley argued that moral judgment amounts to "forming an opinion and expressing it if it is called for." She then added: "Naturally, we ought to avoid forming—and expressing—*crude* opinions. [. . .] But this is a different objection. The trouble with crude opinions is that they are crude, whoever forms them, not that they are formed by the wrong people" (71). The same observation could be made substituting other words for "crude"—words such as "authoritarian," "dictatorial," "tyrannical," or "repressive."

20 John Paul II articulates the complementarity of faith and reason as the Catholic university's privileged task "to unite existentially by intellectual effort two orders of reality that too frequently tend to be placed in opposition as though they were antithetical: the search for truth [reason], and the certainty of already knowing the fount of truth [faith]." *Ex corde ecclesiae*, 1.

21 See Pope Benedict XVI, "Three Stages in the Program of De-Hellenization," (Papal Address at University of Regensburg), September 12, 2006. See also Philip A.

Rolnick, *Origins: God, Evolution, and the Question of the Cosmos* (Waco, Tex.: Baylor University Press, 2015), 150ff.

22 Vatican Council II, *Gaudium et spes* (December 7, 1965), 22.

23 As Matt Briel pointed out to us, people like MacIntyre and Newman both talk about the collision and combat between the disciplines with a trust and hope in reconciliation. His point, which is well taken, is that this dialogue is not without conflict and tension that at times seems like warfare, but ultimately and eventually leads to unity.

24 Disciplinary *isolation*: Reluctance to cross disciplinary boundaries or to "cross the aisle" when it comes to shared disciplinary perspectives on the same independent reality (with the implication that each discipline in isolation has only a partial take on *truth*). Disciplinary *fragmentation*: Faculty identifying with professional associations rather with their own universities as centers of knowledge and scholarly advancement.

25 See Pieper, *Leisure: The Basis of Culture,* Chapter Two, for his discussion of *intellectus* as a kind of knowledge.

26 The historian, C. John Sommerville, puts the matter in the following terms: "If our universities are to become more than professional schools, then rationalism needs to be in dialogue with other "traditions of inquiry." For the most important matters in life include such matters as hope, depression, trust, purpose, and wisdom. If secularism purges such concerns from the curriculum for lack of a way to address them, the public may conclude that the football team really is the most important part of the university. But if they are taken up, we will find ourselves using terms that seem to belong in a religious discourse. We have dodged this issue by saying that the true, good, just are all political, meaning that they can't be discussed but only voted on. But

in fact they could be discussed, if our discussions were to recognize a dimension of ultimacy. It will do wonders in drawing attention and respect to our universities." C. John Sommerville, *The Decline of the Secular University* (Oxford: Oxford University Press, 2006), 22.

27   David Brooks, "The Inverse Logic of Life." July 16, 2013. Aspen Ideas Festival, Aspen, Colorado. 55:50. https://www .youtube.com/watch?v=WlJnNRdVHHw.

28   Benedict XVI, Encyclical Letter *Deus Caritas Est* (Dec. 25, 2005), 28.

29   Augustine Di Noia, "Faith Liberates Reason from Its Blind Spots." April 27, 2007. Pontifical Academy of Social Science, http://www.zenit.org/en/articles/on-deus-caritas -est-and-international-charity.

30   Benedict XVI, *Caritas in veritate,* 56.

31   Benedict XVI, *Caritas in veritate,* 56. See also John Paul II, *Ex corde ecclesiae,* 44.

32   St. Augustine, *Confessions,* trans. John K. Ryan (London: Penguin, 1960), X, xxiii, 33.

33   Burtchaell goes on to explain: "The radical disjunction between divine knowledge and human knowledge had been central to classical Reformation thinking, and its unintended outcome was to sequester religious piety from secular learning. The older, pre-Reformation view, that faith was goaded by Revelation to seek further understanding, and that learning itself could be an act of piety—indeed, the form of piety proper to a college or university — succumbed to the view that worship and moral behavior were to be the defining acts of a Christian academic fellowship. Later, worship and moral behavior were easily set aside because no one could imagine they had anything to do with learning." James Burtchaell, *The Dying of the Light: the Disengagement*

of Colleges and Universities from Their Christian Churches (Grand Rapids, Mich.: Eerdmans, 1998), final chapter.

34   One expression of this is found in Beth McMurtrie, "Catholic Colleges Greet an Unchurched Generation," *Chronicle of Higher Education* (October 13, 2014), http://chronicle.com/article/Catholic-Colleges -Greet-an/149327. She states, "Catholic colleges may be uniquely positioned, too, to appeal to the spiritual-but-not-religious crowd."

35   See Jean M. Twenge, *iGen: Why Today's Super-Connected Kids Are Growing Up Less Rebellious, More Tolerant, Less Happy—and Completely Unprepared for Adulthood—and What That Means for the Rest of Us* (New York: Atria Paperback, 2017), 126–132.

36   Glen Tinder, "Can We Be Good Without God?" *Atlantic Monthly* (December 1989): 68–72, 76.

37   Francis Cardinal George, OMI, "Universities that are Truly Catholic and Truly Academic." September 22, 1998. Inaugural Convocation of President and Faculty Members of Chicago Area Catholic Colleges and Universities, http://www3.nd.edu/~afreddos/papers/george2.htm.

38   One of the implications of this relationship between faith and reason is the necessary role of the Church in the university, a point articulated by John Henry Newman. "But perhaps his [Newman's] most arresting claim is that although the university and the Church are distinct, the end of the first that of knowledge of the truth and that of the second, an incorporation into the truth in a life of holiness, still the university cannot fulfill its object without the Church's assistance. Even more striking is his insistence that this assistance is not merely one of adding a religious value to the university's secular identity but rather one of enabling the university to fulfill its specific intellectual mission. But in large measure

... the chief source of the confusion about the work lies in the fact that most readers assume that Newman's principal interest lay in defining the nature of the university when in fact his real concern was to disclose the character of the educated mind." Don Briel, *University and the Church,* ed. R. Jared Staudt (Providence, R.I.: Cluny Media, 2019), 34.

39 T. S. Eliot, *Choruses from the Rock* (London: Faber & Faber, 1934), opening stanza.

40 E. O. Wilson, *Consilience: The Unity of Knowledge* (New York: Penguin, 1998), 294.

41 This point is made with great clarity by John Paul II in *Centesimus Annus*, 36: "In singling out new needs and new means to meet them, one must be guided by a comprehensive picture of man which respects all the dimensions of his being and which subordinates his material and instinctive dimensions to his interior and spiritual ones. . .. Of itself, an economic system does not possess criteria for correctly distinguishing new and higher forms of satisfying human needs from artificial new needs which hinder the formation of a mature personality. *Thus a great deal of educational and cultural work* is urgently needed, including the education of consumers in the responsible use of their power of choice, the formation of a strong sense of responsibility among producers and among people in the mass media in particular, as well as the necessary intervention by public authorities."

42 Jay Woodruff and Sarah Carew Woodruff, *Conversation with Robert Coles* (Jackson: University Press of Mississippi, 1992): 147. See also Walker Percy, *The Second Coming* (London: Macmillan, 1980), 89.

CHAPTER 2

CHALLENGE

A Brief History of the Catholic University

The principles and the institutional expressions of Catholic universities have a rich history. It is a powerful story of vision and grace as well as tension and failure. While we cannot do justice to the complexity of this narrative, this chapter provides the broad outline of what we as leaders in Catholic universities have been given to hold in trust. For if we do not know the shoulders on which we stand, we will fail to know the role we play.

In his seminal reflection on the nature and promise of Catholic higher education, St. John Paul II noted that the university arose from the heart of the Church (*ex corde ecclesiae*), a fact that is lost on most modern people. In the West, universities developed out of the monasteries and cathedral schools in the late eleventh and twelfth centuries, with Bologna as the first university in 1088 and closely followed by the universities

of Paris, Oxford, Salamanca, Cambridge and others.[1]
As intellectual cathedrals, universities shared in the
remarkable confidence of the Catholic faith that truth
cannot contradict truth, and that the human person
was made to know the whole of reality, to be *capax uni-
versi*, "'capable of the whole', able to comprehend the
sum total of existing things."[2]

This educational purpose of the university also displayed a great confidence in the capacity of the human
community, especially when it cooperated with God's
order and grace, to know the fullness of truth. The possibility to explore the unity of truth and not merely rest
in fragments of knowledge, and the conviction that the
truths of faith enhance and complement the discoveries
of reason, formed and sustained the intellectual tradition of Western thought and culture and provided the
justification and foundation of the university system as
we know it.[3]

This confidence on the part of the university in the
unity of knowledge—and in our ability to discover it—
largely came from two sources. The title of Jean Leclercq's insightful book *The Love of Learning and the Desire
for God* captures these sources well.[4] The "love of learning" comes from an understanding of education rooted
in the classical period of ancient Greece (*paideia*) and
Rome (*humanitas*).[5] It is here where the university
received its vision of the liberal arts, which has served
as a bedrock for the university's self-understanding.

For the Greeks and Romans, education was not just a bit of schooling, but rather it "was what made a person human rather than bestial, and civilized rather than barbaric."[6] The Greeks and Romans universalized education, transforming its parochial focus on identifying with and defending one's tribe or race to an exploration of what was authentically human through an education of the arts that free (liberate) people to become who they are meant to be.[7]

The "desire for God" was uniquely institutionalized with the development of the monasteries and their schools in the West largely beginning with St. Benedict of Nursia (480–543). During a time of great instability, the monks sought the essential from the inessential, the lasting from the fleeting, "the definitive behind the provisional."[8] The guide for their search for God, *quaerere Deum,* was the Word, the scriptures, and in particular, the Psalms, as they established a rule of life upon which the institution of the monastery served as a "weathered presence" in a dark age of invasion, destruction, and lawlessness.[9] In their desire and search for God, they also preserved, almost by accident, the classical works from ancient Greece and Rome.[10]

The Greek and Roman development of the liberal arts and their love for learning and the monastic search and desire for God became increasingly integrated in the Cathedral schools that developed in larger urban areas in the Middles Ages. Through a complicated process lasting centuries, the first universities emerged out of the Cathedral schools. They attracted scholars and students from across Europe who organized themselves into self-governing guilds for the pursuit of learning. Universities began to develop a curriculum that drew upon the Greek ideal of education and set it upon a foundation of Christian metaphysics.[11]

These new universities were consumed by an increasing desire for knowledge. They sought and found new and innovative ways in which different approaches to knowledge connected with one another. They developed in deeper and more systematic ways the seven liberal arts called the *trivium* (grammar, logic, rhetoric) and *quadrivium* (geometry, arithmetic, music, and astronomy). Through various discoveries, especially from Islamic sources, "a flood of authors and texts broke upon Europe. Most of Aristotle's writings, some of Plato's dialogues, the works of Euclid in geometry and Ptolemy in astronomy, and a new mathematics with the versatile Arabic number system were now being made available to the West."[12] There was also a renaissance in civil and canon law, especially in Bologna.[13] These discoveries generated intellectual movements that helped the university become one of the most well-respected institutions in the Western medieval world.[14]

Yet, challenges to the university's fundamental purpose and mission soon began to appear in a variety of ways. Like most successful institutions, universities became corrupted by their increasing wealth. Such wealth diverted their energies away from their noble purpose to merely catering to privileged classes, a problem we still have today.[15] But one of the most significant challenges to their purpose resulted from how certain intellectual movements viewed the unity of knowledge and the relationship between faith and reason. Three particular intellectual trends began to unsettle the traditional view of the relationship of faith and reason: the nominalism in the Middle Ages that separated humanity's freedom from humanity's end or *telos*;[16] the Reformation's tendency in the sixteenth century to distinguish in fundamental ways the operations of faith and reason, sometimes to the denigration of the latter; and certain influences of the Enlightenment of the seventeenth and eighteenth centuries that began to divide and separate the worlds of religion and scientific investigation, sometimes to the marginalization of the former. In short, perhaps to oversimplify, zeal to protect God's freedom and human faith from a growing empirical worldview did not lead to a détente between faith and reason, but to the diminishment of faith and ultimately the loss of confidence in reason itself.

By the nineteenth century, then, the classical emphasis on the unity of knowledge expressed in the tradition of the liberal arts began to be replaced by an emphasis on the specialized knowledge of the new sciences toward the development of the research

university. While the research university brought many
benefits, it also brought a growing assumption that
religious faith was no longer to be considered a form
of knowledge, but rather only an expression of private
piety—an assumption aided in some cases by theologians themselves. This assumption incrementally led
to the removal of theology from the university curriculum, first in Europe and slightly later in the United
States. Philosophy, meanwhile, increasingly called into
question its own capacity to provide stable access to
truth, devolving into ever-more specialized or esoteric
arguments. All these changes led increasingly to the
development of a new epistemology that reduced truth
to what was measurable, quantifiable, and instrumental, and assigned the realms of religion and metaphysics
to private values or opinions.

John Henry Newman sounded an alarm in 1852
when he insisted that the exclusion of theology from
the university would not leave merely a vacuum (the
absence of one particular intellectual claim) but instead
would produce a disorder within the university, as the
mutual relations among the various disciplinary perspectives were no longer properly ordered to the others.[17] Newman noted that all disciplines were *partial*
in their account of complex realities. Nonetheless, the
university of the nineteenth century continued moving
in the direction of specialized and applied knowledge
that offered useful solutions to immediate material

problems, rather than engaging the pursuit of knowledge for its own sake, which had been the great boast of
the so-called pre-modern university.

In addition, the separation of the claims of religion
from the domain of knowledge took place not only in
new secular institutions such as the land grant colleges,
but also in American Protestant higher education.
Incrementally, these Christian universities marginalized religion from the life of the university, relegating
it to isolated schools of divinity and chapel services
that exercised increasingly less influence on the claims
of other disciplines. What seemed like a series of small
changes in fact became a total marginalization with
remarkable effect. Who today would know that the
University of Chicago and Brown University began
as vibrant Baptist institutions, or that the University
of Southern California, Duke University and Boston
University were once deeply Methodist in their institutional commitments?[18]

As a result, a pattern of fragmentation was built into
the institutional structure of the university, one that
changed its basic self-understanding from a unified
project into that of the so-called *multiversity*, or what
the longtime president of the University of Chicago,
Robert Maynard Hutchins, famously called a series
of isolated buildings held together by a central heat-
ing system.[19] Assumptions once so important to the
Catholic intellectual tradition—such as the idea that

to know any one thing required a knowledge of many things, and that the claims of faith and reason needed to be understood in the context of their ultimate complementarity—gradually disappeared.

American Catholic universities at first resisted this innovation and further consolidated their institutional self-understanding in the emerging neoscholastic tradition of the early to middle twentieth century; but all the momentum was on the side of the new utilitarian assumptions concerning the proper business of academia, and the neoscholastic synthesis faded in influence after the Second Vatican Council and the upheavals of the 1960s and 1970s. The modern university, whether Catholic or secular, was now committed to the pursuit of useful knowledge and thus to career preparation and the development of specialized research in increasingly narrowly defined disciplines and sub-disciplines.

These changes in the university had multiple and, in many respects, contradictory consequences that resulted in either an autonomous and fragmented education or an ideologically rigid one.

In terms of its liberal autonomy, the traditional emphasis on the formation of the whole person, a formation not merely of the intellect but also of virtue, was gradually jettisoned in favor of an emphasis on the specialized interests and autonomous choices of students as consumers of knowledge. The entire university was now divided, indeed fragmented, into discrete units of supervision amid which the very language of formation was abandoned. Students were now encouraged to make "educated" choices.[20] Many results followed: faculty members were no longer expected to introduce students to moral reflection; "student services" took on the role of residence life in isolation both from intellectual and spiritual formation; and the chaplaincy was cut off from all other aspects of university life. Students were not expected to gain a sense of the whole of reality within these fragmented experiences, but instead were left to their own resources to keep some sort of balance among them. The classical expectation (based upon the assumption of the unity of knowledge) that the purpose of the university was to assist students to see things in relation to one another and to integrate all aspects of learning and life, simply faded. As a former dean of Harvard College, Harry R. Lewis noted, "Harvard willingly surrendered its moral authority to shape the souls of its students. Harvard wants students to be safe and healthy, but security and safety are the limits of its ambitions. Harvard articulates no ideal of what it means to be a good person, as opposed to a well person."[21] Of course, this problem is not unique to Harvard, and it has manifested itself increasingly in Catholic higher education, especially in areas of student life.

Ironically, this move to liberal autonomy has given rise to an illiberal liberalism in the university. Safety and health have led to "safe spaces" and "trigger warnings" that simultaneously insulate students from debate and promote a fierce agenda of victimization of groups based on race, ethnicity, gender, and sexual orientation as well as on equality of outcome, sexual self-creationism, and other modern ideologies. Failure (by faculty or students) to submit to the dictates (doctrinal norms) of this ideology can have severe consequences, such as labels of bigotry and academic marginalization. This is another example of the deleterious effects on our political culture of a lack of commitment to truth (and ultimately justice)—suspecting (and accusing) those who reject its more radical forms.

Our current situation in light of the Catholic intellectual tradition of education causes us to reflect on a fundamental question. Dante argued in the *Convivio* that young people at the age of late adolescence were uniquely disposed to a transforming educational experience, one that he associated with a "stupor" or astonishment of mind falling upon them in the encounter with great and wonderful things. Such a "stupor," he said, produced two effects: it gave rise to a sense of reverence and receptivity, and it provoked a keen desire to know more. A noble awe was engendered, and studiousness came to life. So the question is: Can the modern university's emphasis on change, utility, therapy, and ideology invite this great-souled transformation? Experience suggests that, without a deeper vison of itself, it cannot.

Alasdair MacIntyre has noted that many of the crises of the last fifty years have arisen from the faulty and disordered judgments of graduates of the most prestigious universities of the West. One thinks of the 2008-09 financial crisis in which some of the brightest technicians and finance specialists engineered the world economy to a near disaster. The same is true of political scientists and foreign policy experts who continued to insist that an understanding of religion was not necessary to evaluate developments in the Middle East or in Africa, a failure with enormous and continuing consequences for a right understanding of cultural and political realities in those regions of the world. Modern culture stresses the central importance of cultural diversity, but often fails in practice to apply it in analyzing specific cultural realities.[22]

These converging developments have brought about the contemporary crisis of the university, for it has become increasingly unclear whether an education that has lost its contemplative and integrative dimensions can be successful in developing virtuous citizens or genuinely competent professionals. The current "education bubble" so often talked about should not be understood primarily in terms of the economic unsustainability or lack of efficiency of the contemporary university system, but rather in terms of its fundamental incoherence, an incoherence that can only be alleviated by a contemplative outlook that discovers and receives rather than manipulates and changes a created universe.

The history of the university and its multiple challenges are far more extensive than can be captured in this short chapter. Yet, for leaders of Catholic universities, the re-appropriation of the basic principles upon which the intellectual project of the university was founded, namely the unity of all knowledge and the complementarity of faith and reason, serves as the *sine qua non* strategy for renewal. If Catholic universities are to go forward at all—and more importantly as Catholic and as intellectually coherent—they will need to reclaim these two fundamental principles in creative and innovative ways. The mission of imparting a habit of wisdom to students, of establishing, in Newman's phrase, a "university in the mind," one entirely consistent with the deep-rooted purpose of the Catholic university, has become a countercultural ideal, considering the changes of the last three centuries. Catholic university leaders need to think with clarity and alertness about their institutions and their profession, lest they slide toward the reigning cultural model, and see their work fall into the intellectual and moral incoherence that has befallen their secular counterparts.

This presents a particular challenge for leaders of Catholic universities whose fundamental purpose they have been asked to hold in trust. If the faculty, administrators, and trustees of a Catholic university are to rediscover its purpose, they will need habits of mind that are historical, philosophical, and theological as well as institutional and practical. They do not have to be professional historians, philosophers, or theologians; but they do need to attend intelligently to the roots of their educational enterprise if they wish to see it succeed and fulfill its true mission.

Chapters One and Two have portrayed the distinctive and defining purpose embedded in a historical narrative that we maintain is faithful to what it means to be a Catholic university. It is in light of this purpose and historical perspective that we see a particular leadership problem in Catholic universities that we call *teleopathy*.[23] It is to this problem of the Catholic university that we now turn in Chapter Three.

ENDNOTES

1   For further information on the medieval university and its origins see Lowrie J. Daly, SJ, *The Medieval University 1200–1400* (New York: Sheed and Ward, 1961). See James Axtell, *Wisdom's Workshop: The Rise of the Modern University* (Princeton University Press, 2016). See also John Henry Cardinal Newman, *Historical Sketches Vol. III, "Rise and Progress of Universities"* (London: Longman's Green and Co., 1924), 1–251. See H. I. Marrou, *A History of Education*

in Antiquity (Madison, Wisc.: The University of Wisconsin
Press, 1956), for the ancient and early medieval influences
of education on the West. For a short history of Western
education see Habiger Institute for Catholic Leadership,
The Heart of Culture: A Brief History of Western Education
(St. Paul, Minn.: Cluny Media, 2020), https://www.stthomas
.edu/media/catholicstudies/center/ryan/publications
/publicationpdfs/The-Heart-of-Culture.pdf

2   Josef Pieper, *Leisure: The Basis of Culture* (South Bend, Ind.:
St. Augustine's Press, 1998), 23–24. This sense of the whole
is often described in terms of the complementarity of the
head and the heart, the contemplative and the active, the
cognitive and the affective.

3   John Paul II reaffirms the Church's "conviction that the
human being can come to a unified and organic vision of
knowledge" John Paul II, Encyclical Letter *Fides et ratio*
(September 14, 1998), 85.

4   Benedictine monk Jean Leclercq provides a helpful distinc-
tion between the *scholastic* method of education focused
on what might be called critical thinking or rationalistic
focusing on questions, disputations, evidence, counter-
points, overall more impersonal and cognitive and the
monastic approach to education that is contemplative,
affective, receptive, poetic, romantic, principally focusing
on our search for God, the role of desire and of the heart.
Jean Leclercq, OSB, *The Love of Learning and the Desire
for God* (New York: Fordham University Press, 1961), 4–6.
John Henry Newman refers to the saints to capture the role
of religious orders on education in the West: St. Benedict
taught *poetically*, St. Dominic taught *scientifically*, and St.
Ignatius of Loyola taught *practically*. A special thanks to
Russ Hittinger who pointed this out to us.

5   See Pope Benedict XVI, "Three Stages in the Program
     of De-Hellenization," (Papal Address at University of
     Regensburg), September 12, 2006, where he argues for the
     importance of Greek influences in Western Culture and
     Christianity in particular.

6   Habiger Institute for Catholic Leadership, *The Heart of
     Culture*, 22.

7   Habiger Institute for Catholic Leadership, *The Heart of
     Culture*, Chapter 1.

8   Pope Benedict XVI, *Meeting with Representatives from the
     World of Culture*, September 12, 2008.

9   Hugh Heclo, *On Thinking Institutionally* (Boulder, Colo.:
     Paradigm Publishers, 2006), 127.

10   "The long and distinguished history of Benedictinism has at
     times been almost coterminous with the history of Europe.
     . . . Benedictine monasticism has often been credited with
     saving for the West the intellectual and cultural heritage of
     the ancient world. It is true; but it is also true that conserv-
     ing the treasures of a civilization was nowhere on the list of
     what Benedict originally hoped to accomplish. He and his
     followers were fleeing the world to contemplate the things of
     heaven and to serve their fellow men through prayer. They
     purposely left behind all ambition for this-worldly influence.
     Yet by a kind of happy accident, the inherent human solidity
     and spiritual strength of the monastery brought it to a place
     of economic, cultural, and spiritual prominence such that for
     some six centuries monasteries would be the beating heart of
     Western cultural life." Habiger Institute for Catholic Leader-
     ship, *The Heart of Culture*, 40.

11   This integration was not easy. "Augustine's [354–430] expe-
     rience might stand for the challenge of the Christian world
     as a whole in attempting to digest and integrate the Greek

ideal. Given fallen human nature, the cultivation of human
excellence was an inherently dangerous activity that could
easily lead to the worst of sins: pride. Jerome, the scholar
and contemporary of Augustine who translated the Greek
Septuagint into Latin, once wrote of a harrowing dream
about his final judgment that had caused him great fear.
'Suddenly I was caught up in the spirit and dragged before
the judgment seat of the Judge; and here the light was so
bright, and those who stood around were so radiant, that I
cast myself upon the ground and did not dare to look up.
Asked who and what I was I replied: 'I am a Christian.' But
He who presided said: 'Thou liest, thou art a follower of
Cicero and not of Christ. For 'where thy treasure is, there
will thy heart be also.''' "Monasticism and the Carolingian
Renaissance," Chapter 4 of Habiger Institute for Catholic
Leadership, *The Heart of Culture*, 37.

12   Habiger Institute for Catholic Leadership, *The Heart of
     Culture*, 46.

13   Daly, *The Medieval University: 1200-1400*, 17.

14   Clark Kerr noted that of the eighty-five institutions in the
     West established by 1520 that still exist, seventy of them are
     universities. Kerr, *The Uses of the University* (Cambridge,
     Mass./London, UK: Harvard University Press, 2001), 152.

15   Universities need wealth to develop, but it is often wealth
     that so easily disorders its purpose. As an old friend of
     ours, Jean Loup Dherse, once said to us: "If you want to
     kill something deprive it of money. If you want to corrupt
     something flood it with money." "During the period from
     the fourteenth to the eighteenth century, universities, like
     other successful corporations, became part of the system
     of estates. Professors claimed hereditary privileges for their
     posts, using their positions like patrimonies and gaining

income from fees, bribes, and even moneylending. Some of them became very rich, and in the carefully graded social hierarchy of the time their status tended to be equated with that of knights. A development that particularly affected the universities of Paris, Oxford, and Cambridge was the rise of colleges. These were originally charitable foundations serving as hostels for needy scholars, but they soon came to be used for academic lectures. (In this way, for example, the Paris faculty of theology and, later, the university as a whole became identified with the college founded in 1253 by Robert de Sorbon.) In the fourteenth- and fifteenth-centuries colleges grew very rich through real estate operations; like some of the monasteries, they became seigneuries ruled by small oligarchies, and these oligarchies dominated the whole university. The colleges monopolized the teaching of the liberal arts and became institutions that catered to the sons of the privileged classes rather than to the international community of scholars." See https://www.encyclopedia.com/social-sciences-and-law/education/education-terms-and-concepts/universities#A

16 For a very accessible introduction to nominalism and its implications for today see George Weigel, "A Better Concept of Freedom" (March 2002), http://www.firstthings.com/article/2002/03/a-better-concept-of-freedom. We touched upon some of these issues in Chapter One. See also Servais Pinckaers, OP, *Sources of Christian Ethics* (Washington, D.C.: The Catholic University of America Press, 1995).

17 John Henry Newman, *The Idea of a University* (Notre Dame, Ind.: University of Notre Dame Press, 1987), first published in 1852.

18 James Burtchaell, *The Dying of the Light: The Disengagement of Colleges and Universities from Their Christian Churches* (Grand Rapids, Mich.: Eerdmans, 1998).

19 Kerr, *The Uses of the University*, 15.
20 David Brooks, "The Organization Kid," *The Atlantic Monthly* (April 2001): 40–54.
21 Harry R. Lewis, *Education without a Soul: How a Great University Forgot Education* (New York: Public Affairs, 2006), 159–160.
22 Alasdair MacIntyre, "The Very Idea of a University: Aristotle, Newman and Us," *New Blackfriars* 91, no. 1031 (2010): 4–19, first published in *The British Journal of Educational Studies* (December 2009). See also Alasdair MacIntyre, "Dangers, Hopes, Choices," in *Higher Learning & Catholic Traditions*, ed. Robert E. Sullivan (Notre Dame, Ind.: University of Notre Dame Press, 2001).
23 Christopher Bartlett and Sumantra Ghoshal, "Changing the Role of Top Management: Beyond Strategy to Purpose," *Harvard Business Review* 72, no. 6 (November-December 1994): 79–88. The challenge here is whether leaders see the problem or not. In their study of Catholic university presidents, Morey and Holtschneider report "lay presidents do not see their lack of religious knowledge and formation as a particular weakness in terms of their own presidency. It is unclear why this is the case. Perhaps critical financial, enrollment, or advancement issues loom so large that the Catholic character and mission of the institution pales in comparison. Some presidents may have compensated for their own limitations in this area by delegating the responsibility to others in the institution. Other presidents may find responsibilities in this area so unspecific and vague that their own limitations pose no real challenge to a sense of professional adequacy. At the same time, some presidents who dismiss a lack of preparation as a negative influence in their own presidency clearly identify it as a problem for Catholic higher education as a whole," Melanie

M. Morey and Dennis H. Holtschneider, "Leadership and the Age of the Laity: Emerging Patterns in Catholic Higher Education," in *Catholic Higher Education: An Emerging Paradigm for the Twenty-First* Century, ed. Anthony J. Cernera (Fairfield, Conn.: Sacred Heart University Press, 2005), 14.

CHAPTER 3

TELEOPATHY

Replacing the Primary with the Secondary

In an address at the University of Notre Dame in 2005, Archbishop Michael Miller, then-secretary of the Congregation for Catholic Education for the Holy See, noted that many presidents as well as trustees and faculty of Catholic universities seemed unaware of the unique advantages of the integral and vibrant Catholic tradition expressed in the two university principles of the unity of knowledge and the complementarity of faith and reason.[1] Twelve years earlier, Michael Buckley, SJ, complained that Catholic universities increasingly have replaced these two principles with a variety of vague moral substitutes. He wrote:

> The "faith that seeks understanding"—what constitutes the substance and richness of the Creed and inspired 2,000 years of Catholic reflection and life—is reduced to a morality or a general social ethic. One looks in

vain for very much beyond American civil religion.
The Catholic, Christian character has shaded off into
a vacuity that offers neither challenge nor much direction to the education given by the institution.[2]

When mission statements, convocation speeches, curriculum reform, research agendas, strategic plans, and
budget priorities mute the university's distinctive primary claims and replace them with secondary claims we
face the leadership problem of *teleopathy*. Combining
the Greek roots *telos* (end or purpose) and *pathos* (disorder or sickness), *teleopathy* refers to an occupational
hazard that often afflicts leaders of institutions, by which
limited goals take on ultimate importance.[3] By overem-
phasizing limited goals, those who suffer from teleopathy
tend to disorder what is primary and secondary, causing
mission drift in their institutions. If there existed a diagnostic manual similar to manuals of medical science
that described the typical pathologies of institutions,
teleopathy, by its frequency and the dangers it poses,
would occupy as central a role in its diagnostic manual
as heart disease or cancer do in medical manuals.

While teleopathy has various and diverse expressions,
it does have a distinct three-stage pattern: Institutional
leaders (1) *fixate* on limited goals and make them ultimate aims. They then (2) *rationalize* these limited goals
as the principal drivers of the institution, and eventually
(3) *detach* their institutions from their fundamental

purposes and "reasons for being." Like most pathologies, teleopathy is easier to see in others than in oneself.
It is not hard to spot it when a company CEO fixates
on wealth maximization alone, rationalizes this on the
basis of the importance of metrics, especially those
that are connected to Wall Street incentives, and then
becomes detached from the deeper goods of the business.[4] The end result is not merely a business whose
practices can be condemned by the wider society; it
sometimes is a business that undermines its own success
in the long run.

Yet the teleopathic pattern can serve as a diagnostic tool for identifying subtler disorders of institutional
leadership. We are using the term here to understand
how faculty, administrators, and trustees of Catholic
universities can *fixate* on secondary goals such as a
generic social ethic, *rationalize* the central importance
of those goals in the name of pluralism and diversity,
and *detach* themselves from the key convictions of
Catholic intellectual life that we described in Chapter
One. All of this results in a serious distortion of the
university's purpose.

TELEOPATHY STAGE ONE: FIXATION ON WHAT IS SECONDARY

There are various reasons why Catholic universities
have moved to articulate their purpose and mission

in terms of a general social ethic. One simple reason
is that articulating epistemological claims as discussed
in Chapter One is more difficult than putting forward
a generic claim to change the world. A second reason
is that every Catholic university *should* educate students to contribute to the common good and be just in
their work, ecologically responsible, and inclusive and
respectful of diversity. These goals play an important
role in the life of a Catholic university, but they are secondary rather than primary principles in relation to its
purpose. Another reason is that the very word "Catholic" itself has become more *divisive* both in regard to
epistemological claims as well as on Catholic moral
stances on marriage, sexuality, and the right to life.[5]
In order to mitigate such conflicts, university leaders
often reduce the university purpose to *selected portions*
of Catholic social thought that appear more acceptable
to the mainstream culture.[6] But even if a Catholic university were to accentuate rather than downplay the
more controversial moral claims of the Church, and
make advocacy of those norms the focus of its mission
statement and strategic goals, this, too, could be putting
as primary something that is secondary to the mission
of a university.

We need to be clear here that secondary does not
mean unimportant, but ordered to the university's
principally intellectual endeavor to cultivate habits of
mind to see things in relation to each other and to make

good judgments about the world. Newman explains at the beginning of *The Idea of the University* that the *essence* of the university is "intellectual, not moral," although he goes on to say that the *integrity* of the university demands the moral and the spiritual, especially in relation to the Church.[7] Another way of putting this, especially from a faculty perspective, is that our fundamental goal with students is to pursue with them the truth of things, to expand and enlarge the mind, embracing the truth in its multiform expressions. We are also to care for the souls of our students. In freedom and openness, we are to engage them in moral and spiritual questions. We are called to mentor and counsel as well as give witness to a life of charity and justice. St. Paul VI's line should be engraved on each of our hearts: "Modern man listens more willingly to *witnesses* than to *teachers*, and if he does listen to teachers, it is because they are witnesses."[8] But our first task as a university is intellectual, this is what makes it a university.[9]

So when secondary principles of a Catholic university education replace primary ones, university leaders are then compelled to create a surrogate language that is insufficient to maintain the distinctiveness of a Catholic university.[10] This substitution of secondary matters for primary ones is especially attractive to university leaders because many such moral claims are genuinely important aspirations for their institutions. Yet when they are separated from the contemplative reality of the Catholic intellectual tradition and its foundational principles, they cannot do what they are pressed into service to do, namely, to provide a coherent account of the distinctive purpose of a Catholic university. Concepts of social justice, diversity, rights, and sustainability are found on most college campuses, but without a theological and philosophical root system they become, as we indicated in Chapter One, opportunities for ideological mischief.

Detached from philosophical and theological normative argument, appeals to these often-politicized umbrella concepts (social justice, diversity, rights and sustainability) can act as *obstacles* to truth-seeking rather than pathways to it. They can become what Socrates in his day referred to as sophistry or rhetoric without being grounded in reason.

This is because, when seen in the proper context of the truth, claims of the Catholic intellectual tradition, such moral and social values, however important or lofty, are an *outcome* of a yet deeper purpose, not the *source* of that purpose. To displace distinctive principles of purpose founded on an integrated theological, philosophical, and anthropological account of the whole of reality with a haphazard set of generic moral and social principles dealing with diversity, justice, and ecology will necessarily undermine the intellectual basis of the Catholic university, and hopelessly confuse its purpose.

This cause/outcome relationship was expressed in Vaclav Havel's critique of various international campaigns for human rights. Havel argued that apart from a connection to a deeper cultural reality, claims for human rights were in danger of becoming mere slogans:

> Politicians at international forums may reiterate a thousand times that the basis of the new world order must be universal respect for human rights, but it will mean nothing as long as this imperative does not derive from the respect for the miracle of Being, the miracle of the universe, the miracle of nature, the miracle of our own existence. Only someone who submits to the authority of the universal order and of creation, who values the right to be a part of it and a participant in it, can genuinely value himself and his neighbors, and thus honor their rights as well.[11]

This miracle of Being is a contemplative beholding of the unity of knowledge that brings us to the fundamental recognition that life, nature, and the universe operates on the basis of a logic of gift that is first received.[12] Havel recognized that a vague commitment to rights, or ethics in general, was prone to the "cut flowers syndrome" spoken of earlier. Such isolated moral phrases might look attractive for a short time but severed from their gifted reality expressed through cultural and religious roots, they inevitably wither. They have "no integrating force, no unified meaning, no true inner understanding" to draw upon to sustain themselves.[13] They offer as a foundation for the imposing edifice of Catholic intellectual life only a platform of sand.

TELEOPATHY STAGE TWO: RATIONALIZATION AND ARTICULATION OF SECONDARY FIXATION

There are few leaders in Catholic higher education who would explicitly deny the two pillars of a Catholic university's purpose described above. Yet the articulation of those key principles of identity, whether in convocation speeches, alumni magazines, graduation remarks, or strategic plans, is constantly muted. When dealing with the voluntary muting of their university's fundamental identity, university administrators find it necessary to embark on a process of rationalization. The reason given for their dampened expression and their preference for surrogate language is an appeal to *pluralism*, to an approach that is thought to be more *inclusive* and palatable for the increasingly diverse population being served. Especially as economic pressures grow, marketers and their branding strategies seek to appeal to an ever-larger consumer base to which the university must adapt its public language. A vision informed by the Catholic intellectual tradition appears from such a market-driven perspective to be too religious or too sectarian for today's university stakeholders (students, faculty, donors, and accreditation agencies). It is thought that insisting on a Catholic theological tradition would place the university at a disadvantage both in recruiting faculty and students and in reflecting the diversity of the wider community.

Yet there is an ironic twist to this way of thinking. *While pluralism is the principal rationale for replacing a theological vision of faith and reason with generic moral and social aspirations, it leads to less—not more—pluralism.*[14] As Catholic universities distance themselves from theological categories and their religious faith, they begin to look very much like the rest of the secular academy. If, in the name of diversity and pluralism, Catholic universities fail to articulate the fundamental convictions of their own tradition, then "diversity" and "pluralism" become mere code words for secularized conformity. If institutional pluralism is to be truly valued, Catholic universities must be encouraged to maintain their *distinctive* contribution. None of this means that Catholic universities need to market themselves solely in sectarian terms—"Come here, we're really Catholic!" Beauty, goodness, truth, the unity of knowledge, the meaning of work as a calling beyond a career, the complementarity of faith and reason, the common good and service—these are not sectarian terms, and even students not initially committed to a deep Catholic identity can both find them attractive and benefit from them. Maintaining Catholic distinctiveness is not a short-term PR strategy—it is a long-term plan whose fruits will produce a vibrant institution, capable of attracting students because of its excellence both in terms of academic mastery of disciplines and the relationship and integration of these disciplines with each other.

At the center of the Catholic university project is the assertion that it offers an education in and for truth, and that truth is both identifiable and attainable. This conviction gives the Catholic university its most distinctive features: a bracing hope and confidence arising from the knowledge that we are made for the truth; a great freedom in debating alternative accounts of the truth; and a deep humility in the awareness of the complex unity of reality. It was not accidental that the distinctive intellectual practice of the medieval university was the *disputatio*, the holding of public debates at which every claim was submitted to argumentation by all comers, and a position made its way only by the force of its rationality.

In contrast, the contemporary university often prides itself in its cultivation of *tolerance*—a necessary consequence of the assumption that truth as such is unknowable. All that remains is an acknowledgement of fragmentary, irreconcilable perspectives and subjective opinions which must be tolerated rather than examined or contested. We now face the sad irony that the university may be the last place at which one might encounter a vital debate about the truth—a place where the claims put forward by various parties are not allowed to be subjected to rational argument.[15] As with diversity, so with tolerance: apart from the deeper realities upon which such values depend, these so-called tolerant and diverse places can easily become dominated by slavish conformity and intense *intolerance* of contrary opinions.

TELEOPATHY STAGE THREE: DETACHMENT FROM THE UNIVERSITY'S FUNDAMENTAL PURPOSE

When Catholic universities articulate their purpose using only generic social and ethical categories, they naturally enough hire and reward faculty and staff based on such categories. The inevitable result is a de-emphasis in matters of hiring, curriculum development, research, and personnel rewards on anything that relates distinctively to the Catholic faith. From the perspective of the university's upper administration, this policy has the *apparent* benefit of avoiding any so-called litmus test of orthodoxy or doctrine. It also affirms the modern presupposition that if religion has any role at all in the university's life, it is not to be found in presenting doctrinal truth claims, that is, in the university's intellectual project, but instead in confronting injustices and inequalities according to a vaguely defined humanitarian sensibility.

But whatever advantages this approach to purpose may bring for avoiding conflict in the short term, it has significant consequences for the fundamental integrity and intellectual excellence of the Catholic university. *Detachment from these key principles, the complementarity of faith and reason and the unity of knowledge, means detachment from the Catholic intellectual tradition and ultimately from the heart of the Church itself. It makes impossible the creation of conditions for a serious conversation between faith and reason among the various academic disciplines of the university.*

When faculty and administrators are hired based on a generic ethic or disciplinary excellence alone, two results follow. First, significant conversations about the two pillars of a Catholic university as articulated in Chapter One are eroded. Faculty lose interest in them, and administrators remain focused on urgent details of day-to-day management. When no explicitly religious or doctrinal criteria are influential in hiring and recruiting faculty, the university's relationship to the Catholic intellectual tradition is either reduced to generic platitudes or is viewed as extrinsic to the curriculum and research of the university. Faculty become more loyal to their *disciplines* than to their *university*, since there is nothing substantial that ties the two together.

A second inevitable result of neglecting to hire with (primary) purpose in mind is that the Catholic university becomes disconnected from the Church. As Newman explains in *The Idea of the University,* the Church is necessary for the integrity of the university, not so much to impose an external correction but rather to fulfill its deepest inclinations, to secure the ordered tension of the disciplines within the circle of knowledge, to draw out its most central insights and provide natural knowledge with the supernatural complement of faith.[16] The Church plays an important role in the university regarding doctrine and liturgy in the intellectual life and in forming theological and cardinal virtues in both faculty and students. Catholic doctrines, such as the *Logos* for example, are not arbitrary prejudices or accidental opinions for the Catholic university's intellectual project; they are foundational in a manner analogous to fundamental principles in the secular sciences. Just as one cannot make progress in chemistry without working with the truths expressed in the periodic table and applying them in research, so one cannot gain an integral understanding of the whole of reality without building upon the theological traditions of the faith. For this reason, faculty and administrators, as well as students, need to examine (and if warranted, remediate) their basic understanding of the Catholic intellectual tradition.[17] As we will discuss in the next chapter, this is done not through imposing dictates but in a seminar fashion of discussion, debate, and open exploration.

Once doctrinal matters are marginalized from the university's intellectual life, significant changes begin to occur. Theologians increasingly see their principal vocation as furthering their academic discipline, understood in largely secular terms, rather than as serving the wider Church. They consequently abandon their integrating role in the core curriculum, usually unwittingly assigning themselves to academic oblivion in the process. The presence of priests and religious is seen as unnecessary. Liturgies such as the traditional Mass of the Holy Spirit that for many centuries has opened the academic year are often removed from university events and convocations. The local bishop is seen as having no governing role in or connection to the Catholic university except for the occasional Mass. The university becomes isolated from the spiritual currents that flow through the Church and is forced to look elsewhere for its existential purpose. Connection to the wider Church may linger on in residual form in occasional community outreach or service-learning opportunities, but these have no impact on the life of the university, and in any case are destined to disappear as the logic of the university's choices increasingly makes itself felt.

In addressing this crisis of identity, leaders of Catholic universities would do well to remember a basic leadership principle lucidly articulated by C. S. Lewis in an essay called "First and Second Things." He noted that "[y]ou can't get second things by putting them first; you can get second things only by putting first things first."[18] If we put first things first, second things are "thrown in;" they find their proper place. But if we put second things first, in the long run we lose *both* first things *and* second things. Jesus noted the same principle in the Sermon on the Mount when he told his followers "Seek *first* the Kingdom of God and its righteousness, and all these other things will be given you as well" (Mt. 6:33). When those who lead Catholic universities put primary emphasis on "second things" like diversity and social justice, and ignore the "first things" of a more deeply contemplative beholding of a created reality, they not only lose the possibility of a unified vision of reality and thus the dynamic intellectual and spiritual life of the university, but they create the very conditions that will undermine the social and moral principles they have enthroned as of first importance, such as diversity, justice, and sustainability.[19]

CONCLUSION

The teleopathic pattern we have described often begins with a distancing of religious truths within the university or college's ecclesial tradition in favor of a humanism with broadly acceptable behavioral norms.[20] It then moves to the methodological preoccupations of the disciplines narrowly understood, and eventually ends in paying court to whoever or whatever pays the bills. This pattern suggests that once a faith-based university severs itself from its deepest theological and ecclesial roots, the generic moral aspirations called in to replace them will eventually give way to the intense institutional pressures presented by our utilitarian, careerist, and technological culture.[21]

There are exceptions to and variations on this teleopathic pattern in Catholic universities, but where the pattern operates, secularization seems inevitable. It should be noted that the loss of anything distinctively Catholic often does not come about because leaders of Catholic universities are overwhelmed and need to submit against their will to secular and consumerist forces. When teleopathy is present, it is usually the faculty, senior administrators, and boards of trustees who purposefully distance their institutions from their own vital traditions and embrace in its place a soft values-based ideal, one that has no power to sustain a university's intellectual life, or to keep back the frankly secular forces that have no interest in or patience with anything religious.

Faculty, senior administrators, and trustees, as the stewards of Catholic universities, must come to terms with the cultural environment that has developed during the last fifty years, especially as it has hold upon Catholic institutions. This does not mean that faculty and administrators of such institutions should downplay their ethical and social commitments, nor does it mean that they should speak only in theological categories and ignore the reality of a pluralistic society.

Roots do not always have to be explicitly recognized. The Catholic university *does* have moral and social convictions and it *must* speak, as it always has, in a language that is intelligible and accessible to those who do not share those convictions. But if *sectarianism* is not a viable option, neither is *assimilation*. The Catholic university must fight against the strong current of mission drift by finding creative ways to more effectively institutionalize the insights of its long history found in the Catholic intellectual tradition. It is to the challenge of institutionalization that we now turn.

ENDNOTES

A shorter essay that focuses on the issues in this chapter was published by the present authors in *America Magazine*, "Our Reason for Being: Restoring the Pillars of Catholic Education" (February 1, 2016), https://www.americamagazine.org/issue/our-reason-being.

[1]   Michael J. Miller, "Challenges Facing American and European Catholic Universities: A View from the Vatican," *Nanovic Institute for European Studies at University of Notre Dame* (October 31, 2005, revised November 14, 2005): 7.

[2]   Michael Buckley, SJ, "The Catholic University and Its Inherent Promise," *America* 168, no. 19 (May 29, 1993): 14: http://www.bc.edu/content/dam/files/offices/mission/pdf1/cu24.pdf. For a powerful analysis of the nature and purpose of the Catholic university see Fr. Michael Buckley's text *The Catholic University as Promise and Project*

(Washington D.C.: Georgetown University Press, 1998).

3   Kenneth Goodpaster, "Ethical Imperatives and Corporate Leadership," *Ethics in Practice: Managing the Moral Corporation.* ed. Kenneth R. Andrews (Boston: Harvard Business School Press, 1991), 217. Goodpaster explains that teleopathy is "a habit of character that values limited purposes as supremely action-guiding, to the relative exclusion not only of larger ends, but also moral considerations about means, obligations, and duties." He goes on to explain that "The manifestations of teleopathy are the manifestations of a decision maker that has sacrificed perspective and balance to a goal or a series of goals over time. . . . By turning over balanced judgment to the pursuit of purpose, purpose becomes a kind of idol. Teleopathy can thus be seen as a secularized form of idolatry." See also the entry "Teleopathy" in the *Blackwell Encyclopedic Dictionary of Business Ethics,* ed. Patricia Werhane and R. Edward Freeman (Oxford: Blackwell Publishers, 1997), 627–628.

4   For a rich description of these goods of business see the Dicastery for Promoting Integral Human Development, *Vocation of the Business Leader* (2018): https://www.stthomas.edu /media /catholicstudies/center/ryan/publications/publicationpdfs /vocationofthebusinessleaderpdf/FinalTextTheVocation- oftheBusinessLeader.pdf.

5   James Heft points to a similar problem when faculty, administrators, and trustees emphasize the so-called small "c" rather than the capital "C" of Catholicism. As Heft points out, "[i]n this practice, the small "c" focuses on ideas most everyone will find acceptable: the dimension of Catholicism that is all-inclusive, that affirms a both/and approach, celebrates the value of reasoning (the natural law tradition) and themes related to creation. In doing so, such people feel

they are able to avoid what appear to them as the sharper
and less attractive aspects of Catholicism, namely the mag-
isterium, dogmas, moral teachings on homosexual acts and
contraception that seem increasingly hard to defend, and
the proclamation of Jesus as one's Lord and Savior. I understand why people feel the need to emphasize the small "c."
However, I simply want to say that without the big "C", the
small "c" will soon become Christian values, and before
long a bland humanism, and eventually all that is truly
distinctive of Catholicism will likely disappear." James L.
Heft, "The Mission of the Faculty," *Boston College's Institute
for Administrators in Catholic Higher Education* (July 13,
2005): 8–9.

6   Within a Catholic perspective, a challenge for any ethic
is how do we see the whole—how to create an ethic that
takes in the whole book of life that fosters integral human
development? We are always in danger of extolling some
principles and virtues at the expense of ignoring others.
We can speak of life, family values and chastity and neglect
structural injustice, global poverty, and pollution. We can
also advocate solidarity with the poor and environmental sustainability while failing to recognize the too often
bankrupt notion of sexuality that is reduced to safety and
consent. Within the university, the more likely tendency
is to find the Church's social teaching attractive and progressive, while her life and sexual ethic are seen as back-
ward and regressive. Rabbi Jonathan Sacks, former Chief
Rabbi of the United Hebrew Congregations of the Com-
monwealth, captures this sentiment more generally when
he writes: "We have lost our traditional sense of morality. I
do not mean that we are less moral than our grandparents.
We care about things they hardly thought about: world

poverty, inequality, global warming and the loss of biodiversity. We are more tolerant than they were. But note this: the things we care about are vast, distant, global, remote. They are problems that require the coordinated action of millions, perhaps billions of people. The difference we as individuals can make to any one of them is minimal. That does not mean they are not important: they are. But they are issues of politics, not of morality in the conventional sense. When it comes to personal behaviour we have now come to believe that there is no right and wrong. Instead, there are choices. The market facilitates those choices. The State handles the consequences, picking up the pieces when they go wrong. The idea that there may be things we would like to do and can afford to do but which we should not do, because they are dishonourable and a betrayal of trust, has come to seem outmoded," (Rabbi Sacks, "Without a shared moral code there can be no freedom in our society," June 26, 2009): http://rabbisacks.org/without-shared-moral-code -can-freedom-society/).

7   John Henry Newman, *The Idea of a University* (Notre Dame, Ind.: University of Notre Dame Press, 1987), ix.

8   Pope Paul VI, Encyclical Letter *Evangelii Nuntiandi* (December 8, 1975), 41.

9   John Henry Newman defines the focus of the university in the preface to *Idea of a University* in the following way: "The view taken of a University in these Discourses is the following: That it is a place of *teaching* universal *knowledge*. This implies that its object is, on the one hand, intellectual, not moral; and, on the other, that it is the diffusion and extension of knowledge rather than the advancement... Such is a University in its *essence*, and independently of its relation to the Church. But, practically speaking, it cannot

fulfil its object duly, such as I have described it, without the Church's assistance; or, to use the theological term, the Church is necessary for its *integrity*. Not that its main characters are changed by this incorporation: it still has the office of intellectual education; but the Church steadies it in the performance of that office." John Henry Newman, *The Idea of a University* (London: Longmans, Green, and Co., 1907), ix.

10   Moving to the lowest common denominator tends to flatten identity and mission. One example of this is found in the case of the College of Santa Fe, a Catholic Lasallian school that found itself negotiating with a secular New Mexico University to be acquired because of its serious financial trouble. When asked about the relationship of its Catholic identity in such a sale to a secular university, Stuart Kirk, Santa Fe's president, responded, "There is nothing that is part of this school that is uniquely Catholic. . . .We certainly have a long history of Lasallian traditions, which are things like being student-centered and having community involvement, and I think if you looked at those you would assume any honorable school adheres to those traditions." Jack Stripling, "Keep Santa Fe Weird," *Inside Higher Ed* (2008): https://www.insidehighered.com /news/2008/12/15/keep-santa-fe-weird. A Catholic college or university that severs itself from its uniquely theological and ecclesial roots and reduces it mission to generic but important qualities such as student centered, community involvement, values based, justice oriented, etc. may have distinctive elements of a Catholic college, but it will not be, as Kirk points out, uniquely Catholic.

11   Vaclav Havel, "The Miracle of Being: Our Mysterious Interdependence," reprinted from *Sunrise Magazine*, (Theo-

sophical University Press, 1994): http://www.theosophy-nw
.org/theosnw/issues/gl-hav1.htm.

12 Benedict XVI, Encyclical Letter *Caritas in veritate* (June
29, 2009), 5. As we have repeated several times in this
text, Benedict states that "the logic of gift does not exclude
justice, nor does it merely sit alongside it as a second element added from without; on the other hand, economic,
social and political development, if it is to be authentically
human, needs to make room for the *principle of gratuitous-
ness* as an expression of fraternity" (36).

13 Havel, "The Miracle of Being: Our Mysterious Interdependence," paragraph 8.

14 When the University of St. Thomas (Minn.) began to
explore the possibility of starting a new law school, it initially argued that its distinctive mission would be characterized as a "values-based law school." This so-called
distinctive quality brought scorn from the other three law
schools in the Twin Cities area who sardonically responded,
"So we are values-less law schools?" This exchange brought
into clarity that "values-based" or "ethics-based" added little by itself to the discussion of mission, since every institution values something. Soon after the law school began to
describe itself as a "faith-based" law school.

15 For one expression of this problem, see Judith Shulevitz,
"In College and Hiding from Scary Ideas," *New York Times*
(March 21, 2015): http://www.nytimes.com/2015/03/22
/opinion/sunday/judith-shulevitz-hiding-from-scary
-ideas.html?_r=0.

16 Don Briel, *University and the Church,* ed. R. Jared Staudt
(Providence, R.I.: Cluny Media, 2019), 44-45.

17 It is important to note, however, that the Catholic intellectual tradition cannot be disconnected from the Church.

John Cavadini, a theologian from the University of Notre
Dame, warns of the dangers of abstracting this intellectual
tradition from a living relationship with the institutional
Church; otherwise, it meanders into Gnosticism. This
"Gnosticized version" of the Catholic intellectual tradition
cultivates "an intellectual tradition in which 'Catholic' is
not normed by accountability to any incarnate historical
body but only to the disincarnate, a-historical church of
the mind." Cavadini argues that the Catholic intellectual
tradition is that incarnational expression of the mind of
the Catholic community, the Church, and is expressed in
the ongoing pursuit of the exploration and development of
Catholic thought and culture. He is concerned about recent
attempts of certain Catholic universities to define their
Catholic claims not in their relationship to the Church—
that living incarnational, historical mystery overseen by
the apostolic claims of often very human and sometimes
poorly educated bishops—but rather in a relationship to
the Catholic intellectual tradition, an idealized, gnostic
alternative of our own invention" (John C. Cavadini, "Open
Letter to the University Community," *The Observer* (April
19, 2006). https://ndsmcobserver.com/2006/04/open-letter
-to-the-university-community/). We are grateful to Matt
Briel who reminded us of this point in our editing process.

18 C. S. Lewis, "First and Second Things," in *C.S. Lewis First
and Second Things,* ed. Walter Hooper, (Glasgow: Collins
Fount Paperbacks, 1985), 22.

19 Principles such as diversity, justice, hospitality, and the common good are important to university education, but we
cannot get more out of these principles than they are able to
give. Diversity, as important as it is for societies and institutions, cannot serve as a primary principle for a university.

When it is placed as a primary principle it will lead either
to anarchy (diversity for its own sake) or it will become a
pretext for imposing an ideology of conformity. As many
critics have noted, universities are now tending toward the
latter. Universities often have little diversity of thought and
have created their own doctrinal litmus tests that have been
more controlling and dogmatic than most fundamentalist
churches. As New York Times columnist Nicholas Kristoff
put it, the notion of diversity popular in academia means
that we "welcome people who don't look like us, as long
as they think like us." Nicholas Kristoff, "The Dangers of
Echo Chambers on Campus," *New York Times* (December
10, 2016): https://www.nytimes.com/2016/12/10/opinion
/sunday/the-dangers-of-echo-chambers-on-campus.html.

20   Burtchaell, *The Dying of the Light* (Grand Rapids, Mich.:
     Eerdmans, 1998).

21   For a description of the increasingly technological culture
     we are living in, see Russell Hittinger, "Technology and
     the Demise of Liberalism," Chapter Ten of *The First Grace*:
     Rediscovering the Natural Law in a Post-Christian World,
     ed. Jeremy Beer (Wilmington, Del.: ISI Books, 2003).

CHAPTER 4

INSTITUTIONALIZING

Passing on the Fire of Mission and Identity

If faculty, senior leaders, and trustees are to avoid the pathology described in Chapter Three, they need to think and act institutionally, *passing on the fire* of the university's Catholic mission and identity. The basic idea behind "institutionalizing" is attention to the dynamic incentives of the organization which need to be mutually reinforcing and which can work *against* one another if they are not harmonized.[1]

Managing organizations is in many ways like managing ecosystems. As environmentalists often remind us, "everything is connected to everything else." Incentive systems, for example, designed to achieve a high ranking in *U.S. News and World Report* can have significant (and unintended) side effects in relation to an institution's core mission. In a Catholic university, the direction given by its leadership influences the seriousness with which faculty, staff, and students interpret the espoused principles of the institution. Rankings should function for universities like profits should function for corporations—as metrics of success, not as ends in themselves.

It is important to remember that *there are two languages of mission in every organization.* There is the *aspirational* language articulated in mission statements, and there is the language of *practice* or "*values-in-action*" driven by the incentives, rewards, hiring, and promotion systems of the organization. When the two come into conflict, the second language inevitably prevails. A significant gap between the two languages of mission is a sign of what might be called "institutional hypocrisy" (a disconnect between institutional "talk" and institutional "walk"), a problem that may emerge even when it is not intended.

INSTITUTIONALIZING

A thorough approach to the institutionalization of the primary principles for a Catholic university would attend to the many variables indicated in the figure below with an eye to their mutual reinforcement and their ultimate support of the university's superordinate goals (institutional purpose): *strategic* planning; *structures* of the board of trustees, colleges, schools and departments of the university, centers and institutes,

and student and residential life; departmental annual performance evaluation and reward *systems*; *staff* hiring and student admissions; critical *skill* models in each discipline; and the cultural *style* of interactions among administrators, faculty, and students. For present purposes, we will focus on four areas: recruitment and hiring (which involve *systems, staff*, and *structure*); faculty/leadership formation (which involves *staff* and *systems*); new and innovative programs to better foster the two principles identified in Chapter One (which involve *structure* and *staff*); and university governance (which involves *strategy* and *structure*).[2] These serve as four important levers for institutionalizing mission and identity (*superordinate goals*).

1. MISSION-DRIVEN RECRUITMENT AND HIRING: ADMINISTRATORS AND FACULTY

The first challenge of institutionalization lies in the process of recruitment and hiring. When it comes to recruiting and hiring faculty and administrators for Catholic universities, a typical approach is to appoint a search committee—and in the case of senior leadership positions (president, provost, deans, and upper-level staff administrators) to employ the services of a professional search firm.

Appointing search committees can be challenging in faith-based and mission-guided schools because the natural tendency in selecting search committee members is to choose a "representative" group to avoid concerns about bias within the university community. The result is a diversity in relation to discipline, gender, age, and faculty/staff/student status. Then, as the search committee assembles for the first time and is charged with its task, it is common to lay out the *attributes* that the group will be seeking as it reviews dossiers that will be presented by candidates. These attributes are translated into a *position description* and sent out through appropriate media and compared with *the database of the search firm* if one is used. The search committee then develops a set of interview questions and often allocates these questions to its individual members so that interviews can be coordinated and comparable among the finalist candidates.[3]

A search process designed in this way is problematic if the intention of the university or college or department is to strengthen and support the Catholic mission and identity of the institution. For one thing, the criteria for the selection *of the search committee* should mirror the criteria being sought *among the candidates themselves*. Otherwise, the likelihood is great that a "least common denominator" screen will be constructed, and the search firm will be given weak instructions that are generic in relation to the institution's core mission. Characteristics like professional competence, problem-solving ability, congeniality, and strong educational motivation practically go without saying. But characteristics like a commitment to the distinctiveness of a Catholic university, the importance of the unity of knowledge, and a conviction about the complementarity of faith and reason—these do *not* go without saying and need to be placed *front and center* before all members of the search committee. This lack of clarity has become a particular problem for hiring presidents of Catholic universities. Melanie Morey and Dennis Holtschneider explain that while boards of trustees:

> have become more proficient in terms of assessing the capacity and fit, of candidates in traditional areas of executive leadership, their expectations regarding

mission and identity leadership have remained vague, unfocused, and largely unarticulated. If the people who hire them remain unable to define appropriate religious qualifications for Catholic college presidents, it is unlikely there will be any consensus about what background should be deemed adequate for these leadership roles. If this lack of clarity among trustees continues, the chances for mission drift only compound.[4]

One small way to explicitly highlight the mission question in the hiring process is to request finalist candidates to read a well-chosen essay on the nature of a Catholic university (or *Ex corde ecclesiae* itself) and be prepared to offer some practical applications of it either to their administrative priorities or to their research, their teaching, and their university service.

Another key part of the recruitment and hiring process is that the *field of recruitment* needs to be thoughtfully determined. How important is it to look *outside* the university for the leadership being sought? Are there not *prima facie* reasons to look for talented and enculturated people *within* the ranks of current administrators and senior faculty, for men and women whose deepest convictions and commitments are demonstrated within the academic community? Many organizations make the mistake of instinctively looking outside for talent that may well be ready and groomed from within. *Succession planning needs to be part of every organization with a culture worth preserving.* Nevertheless, when looking outside the university is prudent, *where* should the search be directed? Toward institutions, presumably, that appear to have strong Catholic cultures responsive to *Ex corde ecclesiae*—not simply toward high profile successful leaders at prestigious secular institutions. The quest needs to be for someone who can help *strengthen* the mission and identity of the university, not simply for someone who brings a successful track record in relation to other, less critical measures.

When it comes to recruiting and hiring faculty, one of the crucial questions is at what level faculty participate in the mission of a Catholic university.[5] It is the *faculty* who ultimately express and define a university's deepest convictions, which is why mission-driven recruitment and hiring is one of the most important policies to institutionalize within an organization. If the recruitment and hiring process at a Catholic university only engages candidates' academic credentials, and nothing is expected in terms of their contribution to *the university's religious intellectual identity*, the secularization of the university is inevitable. There are several such levels to consider: methodological rigor, research creativity, pedagogical excellence, ethical reflection, engagement with the religious mission of the institution, and identification with the Catholic mission of the university. We offer below one way to think through a faculty recruitment/hiring strategy for a Catholic university that considers various levels in which people participate in the mission of the institution. The following three levels can entail a variety of initiatives, each of which is incomplete in isolation from the others and which, if not taken as a whole, can cause serious distortions and ill-will.[6]

A *Hiring Teachers and Scholars of Excellence*: A mission-driven hiring strategy should seek to attract professors to the university who have either a distinguished record of teaching and scholarship or the promise for developing such a record. Possible hires should have a demonstrated respect for and understanding of the distinctive features of the university's Catholic identity, whatever their personal commitment to a faith tradition. As John Paul II indicated, such scholars, even when not committed Catholics, can make a real and essential contribution to the university's mission in the light of their own disciplinary competence and commitment. However, many Catholic universities tend to hire on this level *and this level alone.* Unfortunately, an increasing number of universities will ask interviewees to respond to the mission-driven character of the university, and if the answer is not hostile to its Catholic character, the responses are accepted.

B *Hiring and recruiting scholars from other religious and philosophical traditions:* Catholic universities should seek scholars and teachers from other Christian denominations and faith traditions who have a respect for and knowledge of the fundamental distinctiveness of the Catholic mission of the university, and who can make a contribution to that mission in the light of their own faith and philosophical tradition. It is commonly heard that Lutherans, Jews, Mormons, Hindus, and others are often more engaged in ethical and spiritual questions than many Catholics. A Catholic university should be a place fostering what Pope Francis speaks of as a "culture of encounter," a *dia-logos,* a dialogue with other faith traditions.[7] Faculty who take their religious traditions seriously make an indispensable contribution to Catholic universities precisely in terms of their engagement as non-Catholics. They bring to the university both a fresh set of eyes to its mission and their own distinct insights with which to engage the Catholic tradition.[8] Catholic universities naturally attract people of a wide variety of faith traditions who are interested in ethical and spiritual questions. Such faculty find themselves freer at Catholic universities to raise spiritual, moral, and social questions in their research and teaching precisely because of the mission. Yet this

kind of hiring and recruiting is often not inten-
tional, but only a happy accident. As a result,
attracting people of various faith traditions can
and is easily lost when it is not institutionalized
in the university's hiring strategy.

C *Hiring seriously committed and intellectually
accomplished Catholics who seek a dialogue
between faith and reason*: The Catholic faith is not
merely a private reality; it is a living and organic
reality with a profound intellectual dimension.
This is why it was able to give birth to the university in the first place. Thus, its ecclesial identity, its sacramental life, and its engagement with
the Catholic intellectual and social traditions are
indispensable expressions of the commitments
of a Catholic university.[9] A Catholic university
should provide the freedom and space for Catholic intellectuals to explore the unique contributions of their own tradition. This exploration
does two things simultaneously. Catholic faculty
members can fully commit to the Catholic university's distinctive claim not only to pursue a
free and open search for truth, but also to express
with integrity and conviction a commitment to
the Catholic university's claim to possess and disclose the fount of truth.[10] Precisely because they
are Catholic, they freely commit to the fullness
of a Catholic vision of university life. Second,
Catholic priests, religious and laypeople who are

seriously committed intellectuals and who draw
upon their faith within their academic pursuits
provide an indispensable and unique contribution to further their own discipline by seriously
engaging the resources present in the Catholic
intellectual tradition.

It will be helpful, in this context, to keep in mind
what *Ex corde ecclesiae* asks of Catholic universities:

All teachers and all administrators, at the time of
their appointment, are to be informed about the
Catholic identity of the Institution and its implications, and about their responsibility to promote, or at
least to respect, that identity.[11]

And also:

In ways appropriate to the different academic disciplines, all Catholic teachers are to be faithful to, and
all other teachers are to respect, Catholic doctrine
and morals in their research and teaching.[12]

This language is meant to foster and protect the mission and identity of the Catholic university while
making it clear that teachers and administrators who
are not Catholic—but who respect the institution's
Catholic nature—are vital members of the university
community.[13]

To some, the idea that Catholic universities should have a critical mass of Catholic faculty appears exclusive, sectarian, and expressive of religious discrimination. An analogy might help to see the reasonableness and necessity of such a goal for the identity of a Catholic university. Most people would not have a problem with the idea that the NAACP should have a critical mass of African Americans if it is to carry out its mission successfully. Racial identity in this case is not incidental; without maintaining such a critical mass of people of color within its organization, there is a good chance that the NAACP would lose its distinctive identity. In a similar way, a Catholic university and its programs cannot be faithful to the university's mission without Catholics who take their faith seriously in relation to their respective academic disciplines.[14] The one common position that often still requires being Catholic is the president of the university. It goes without saying that a baptismal certificate alone will not guarantee the protection and development of the Catholic mission and culture of the university, but without the ecclesial and sacramental identification of the president, the relationship to the deepest roots of the university will eventually become distant.

One creative and helpful organizational initiative to address the hiring and recruitment of Catholics within the university has been developed at the University of Notre Dame.[15] In 2008, the Office for Academic Mission Support was created to foster Catholic hiring at Notre Dame. What this three-person office, reporting to the Provost and occasionally to the President, has done is to create a *database* of potential Catholic candidates for future administrative and faculty positions at the university. This database is informational only and consists of curriculum vitae and other documentation of some 33,000 academics, 11,000 of whom are Catholics in the active file (identified in various ways including voluntary self-identification on applications, word of mouth recommendations, or various statistically significant indices of Catholicism). This information is shared with deans of colleges at Notre Dame when positions are approved for hiring. The intention is to help the various units of the university to *search* rather than simply *sift* applicants in the hiring process with an eye to a central part of its Mission Statement:

> The intellectual interchange essential to a university requires, and is enriched by, the presence and voices of diverse scholars and students. **The Catholic identity of the University depends upon, and is nurtured by, the continuing presence of a predominant number of Catholic intellectuals.** This ideal has been consistently maintained by the University leadership throughout its history.[16]

The efforts of the Office for Academic Mission Support have shown signs of significant influence, albeit influence of a non-directive kind, since the role of this initiative is to expand the pool of candidates. The Office does not restrict or select candidates. Since the Office's inception, the number of faculty hired at Notre Dame has increased, and importantly, the *percentage* of Catholic faculty has increased at the same time.[17] This approach is *creating the conditions for success* in hiring seriously committed and intellectually accomplished Catholics who seek a dialogue between faith and reason, which advances the purpose of the university and mitigates the increasing pressures of secularization within the academy.

Hiring the right faculty is a complex task. Notre Dame's initiative to create a database of Catholic scholars is one factor in the recognition of a multifaceted strategy reflected in the kind of faculty a Catholic university should be hiring. The initiative gives the schools and departments a pool of Catholic candidates that often they would otherwise not be aware of, but it leaves to the school and department the freedom to judge based on the variables of who is available, which person would be best, what is needed in the school and department and so forth.[18]

Let us conclude with two final observations related to this complex task of hiring and recruitment. First, an increasing number of Catholic universities hire to foster greater racial, ethnic, and gender diversity among their faculty and staff. This is an important strategy for multiple reasons, but if this diversity approach is not situated *within* a mission-driven strategy, there is no guarantee that the Catholic mission and identity will be nurtured and protected. Actually, the danger of placing diversity as the main goal of hiring and recruitment is that Catholic universities will begin to look like all other universities which have the same strategy.

Second, in connection with faculty recruitment: it is important to actively seek out Catholic scholars to serve as endowed chairs or senior academics in the various departments across the university. Such chairs would be explicitly tasked with fostering the dialogue between faith and various key disciplines throughout the university such as Catholic literature, Catholic social thought in relation to economics, business, or law, theology and science, and so forth. These *thought leaders* would serve as role models to their colleagues—structural reminders of the unity of knowledge and the centrality of the mission.[19]

2. FACULTY AND LEADERSHIP FORMATION

The second challenge of institutionalization centers on faculty and leadership *formation*. Timothy Kirchoff explains:

> [T]he biggest weakness of the recruitment recom-
> mendation as it is usually articulated is its treatment
> of faculty themselves as a *static* quantity when the
> reality is rather more complex: Scholars of every dis-
> cipline and at every stage of their professional devel-
> opment can participate in the unique mission of the
> Catholic university, but are too often left on their
> own to discover how to do so. *Catholic scholars must
> not simply be found but formed.*[20]

Unlike Catholic health care systems, where senior leaders often participate in substantive and systematic leadership formation programs throughout their careers,
there has not been as much formation within Catholic
universities to engage faculty and administrators with
a deeper understanding and commitment to the riches
of the Catholic intellectual tradition. Universities usually do not form and develop their own faculty, except
perhaps in pedagogy and in disciplinary excellence
(although there are significant exceptions). Indeed,
"faculty development" in many Catholic universities
tends to be *remedial* rather than *formative*. There is
seldom a strong incentive structure for the pursuit of
self-development in the areas that make Catholic universities distinctive.[21]

One promising approach to formation is to take
note of the key milestones in a faculty member's participation in the life of the institution (and analogous

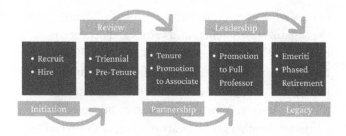

milestones in the life of an administrator). These milestones are: *Initiation* after hiring, *Review* on the path
to tenure, *Partnership* once tenure is achieved, *Leadership* at promotion to Full Professor, and *Legacy* at the
time of retirement (see figure above).[22] Each of these
milestones represents an opportunity to take some
structured retreat time with peers and to reflect on the
purpose of the Catholic university. "What is the role
that each of us is called to play in furthering our institutional vocation? Is my role deepening as I progress
through the ranks and take on more responsibilities (or
pass on my responsibilities to others)? How does the
purpose of the university manifest itself in my teaching,
research, and service?"[23]

MILESTONES IN THE CAREERS OF UNIVERSITY FACULTY

The spirit of such milestone retreats is well articulated by Melanie Morey and Dennis Holtschneider,
CM: "Organizational cultures are kept vibrant by the

energy of a core group who personally identify with the organization's beliefs and values and accept a public role in motivating others to do likewise."[24] Historically, the custodians of the cultures of Catholic universities have been religious orders of men and women (Benedictines, Jesuits, Vincentians, Sisters of Notre Dame, Christian Brothers) or priests in diocesan universities. Today, with the depletion in numbers and influence of these groups, it is essential that lay leaders take greater responsibility. Morey and Holtschneider continue:

> Religious cultures are organizational cultures and operate in the same way. They require a core group of people at the center of the organization whose belief and witness both allows and encourages others to freely express and explore their own religious convictions. If, in the absence of the visible witness of religious congregations, a college desires to manifest a Catholic culture, then it must develop anew that core group within the organization. Knowledge of Catholicism is not enough. Quiet conviction is not enough. (There are Catholics of strong religious conviction teaching in state colleges, and that does not make those colleges Catholic.) Only a core of visible believers, people whose faith is palpable, can leaven the culture of an organization. Any strategy to preserve these cultures, and keep them vibrant over time, must look to create and sustain this core.

Otherwise, these institutions will become secular in all but name and history.[25]

In a non-religious context but in the spirit of Morey and Holtschneider, William W. George comments in his book, *Authentic Leadership,* about the importance of *developing* leaders in institutionalizing core values in organizations:

> When the company's leaders become role models for its values, the impact on the entire organization is tremendous. The trust of the leadership is earned through practicing the company's values every day, not just by espousing them. But when leaders preach one thing and practice another, commitment is quickly lost, and employees become doubly cynical.[26]

The university needs to create a variety of faculty development programs that help to form and sustain faculty as they develop their own roles within the university's Catholic mission. Let us discuss in more detail two of the milestone formation opportunities for faculty indicated above under the headings of *Initiation* and *Partnership/Leadership.*

Initiation. The formation that faculty receive during their doctoral programs and at the beginning of their academic careers is a crucial time for their development. One of Alasdair MacIntyre's grave concerns about new faculty coming out of doctoral programs of research universities is that their formation over the previous five to seven years may have created such specialized minds that they have lost the capacity to see things in relation to each other, to converse with other disciplines, and even to entertain the possibility of a unity of knowledge expressed in Chapter One. What is needed for PhD students and new faculty are interdisciplinary seminars and discussions to engage them in their intellectually formative years with the principles of the unity of knowledge and the dialogue between faith and reason. There are multiple possibilities here.

One important program is how the university orients their new faculty. How it introduces a new faculty member to campus speaks volumes about its commitment to the purpose of the university. Just starting a position is a busy time for faculty—getting courses ready, learning the logistics of the university and getting the general lay of the land. Too often in such crowded schedules, the mission and culture of the university can either get squeezed out or become a topic in the orientation program on some late Friday afternoon. When this happens, a significant opportunity has been squandered.

Especially when faculty are first hired, they are usually most open to connect to the institution and its mission. Failing to make such connections increases the probability of faculty shifting their primary loyalties to their *discipline* and to view their institution as a contract employer—a place where they are paid to teach, but the real work is in the research connected to their discipline. We have found that engaging new faculty in a serious and thoughtful fashion with the Catholic intellectual tradition creates the conditions for faculty to embrace the university's mission and culture in a powerful way. We (Goodpaster and Naughton) have given such seminars at our university as well as at others. What we have found is that most faculty are unaware of the intellectual vitality and depth of the university's Catholic intellectual tradition, and they find the tradition more robust than they originally thought.

We have facilitated three- and four-day Catholic Intellectual Tradition (CIT) seminars using a pedagogy based on the Aspen Executive Seminars originally developed by Mortimer Adler.[27] He believed that great texts can generate vibrant and robust conversations on their meaning and their implications. The openness of the seminar process fosters an atmosphere of freedom and inquiry that is appreciated by all. The CIT Seminar is not for "specialists" in theology or philosophy, although a number of them do participate in the program. Nor is the seminar a quick fix to Catholic identity in the university. It proposes no curriculum or research agenda, although discussions and debates over these issues do occur. Rather, the seminar engages enduring texts which both support and challenge the CIT so as to foster personal and institutional reflection on the faculty's vocation as teachers and administrators within Catholic higher education. In order to do this effectively, participants are encouraged to debate, discuss, and bring the fullness of their own experiences to the table as they encounter the Scriptures, Augustine, Aquinas, Newman, Maritain, Dostoevsky, Day, as well as the challengers to this tradition, including Machiavelli, Nietzsche, and Marx.

An important characteristic of the seminar is that it first and foremost builds an intellectual engagement among the faculty. The seminar seeks to provide a community-building experience by connecting new faculty to the mission of the university and to colleagues across the university from other disciplines. While the seminar discusses important ideas, its uniqueness is that it addresses these ideas in terms of the shared purpose of their new institution. This is often the first time for these faculty to engage with colleagues across disciplines on a shared institutional mission.

One final thought on such a seminar: one might think that when discussions of Catholic mission and identity are encouraged, they will become embroiled in various kinds of controversy. Our experience, however, is that while controversy is not avoided, the conversation is text-driven rather than issue-driven, allowing for a more constructive discussion.

Universities also have resources external to themselves to help build an intellectual community. Collegium, which is sponsored by the Association of Catholic Colleges and Universities (ACCU), offers week-long summer seminars on faith and reason, where faculty of various religious backgrounds and disciplines engage the meaning of Catholic higher education in relation to their own vocation as faculty.[28] The Lumen Christi Institute at the University of Chicago in collaboration with other institutions has created a variety of summer seminars aimed at serious dialogue between faith and culture. Seminar topics have included Newman, Catholic social teaching and its relationship to economics, finance and business, faith and science, Augustine, Aquinas, among others. These seminars introduce participants to central themes, figures, and texts from the Catholic intellectual tradition. Without such seminars, people of faith within disciplines never have an opportunity to explore with others what the dialogue between faith and reason can look like. Too often such dialogues are suppressed in disciplines. Stephen Barr, a physicist, who started the Society of Catholic Scientists, thought he was alone in his ideas of the relationship between religion, philosophy, and science. Apparently, he thought, scientists don't discuss religion. Within two years of starting the Society of Catholic Scientists, a thousand members joined. Among the topics they address is the existence and order of the cosmos; God and nature;

primary and secondary causality; the supernatural and miracles; modern physics and natural theology; creation and providence; the beginning of the universe and modern cosmology; God and time; human origins and human distinctiveness; and biological evolution. Faculty in science, especially younger faculty, should be supported, encouraged, and rewarded to participate in such seminars and societies.[29]

Partnership/Leadership. One of the great joys (and sources of relief) for faculty members comes when they receive tenure. While tenure protects the faculty in a variety of ways such as job security and free speech, any relationship fixated only on rights and not on responsibilities will be short-lived. Faculty have the duty to work hard, to speak responsibly, and to play a leadership role in the university. When a university grants tenure it enters a long-term relationship with faculty. The granting of tenure is an important moment for the university to engage tenured faculty as future leaders of the university. Andre Delbecq, who has since passed away, created the Ignatius Faculty Forum at Santa Clara University. He saw the forum as an opportunity to engage those faculty who are tenured in their leadership role at the university within the context of spiritual formation. Delbecq was influenced by his work with Catholic health care, especially his work with Ascension Health. Future leaders of Catholic institutions must be leaders who have a profound spiritual and religious sense in order to connect and guide the spiritual and religious character of the institution. Delbecq explained that "Leadership skills develop primarily through reflection on such actions as engaging decisions, accepting setbacks and reorienting projects, starting endeavors from scratch, turning around failed programs, etc. . . . In like manner, a hallmark of spirituality is discovering God in the busyness of everyday life."[30]

Another effective way to form leaders at the university is to develop programs that provide "immersion opportunities" for faculty. Religious orders can take faculty to the founders' homes such as Assisi (Franciscans), Loyola (Jesuits), or Subiaco or Monte Cassino (Benedictines). At the University of St. Thomas (Minn.), the Office of Mission has developed a year-long seminar for faculty that culminates with a week in Rome where they visit sites such as the Congregation for Catholic Education and the university's Rome campus.

The main point is that, as we have seen, there are different "seasons" in the life of faculty and administrators in Catholic colleges and universities. Support and development are needed for each of these seasons, marked by the milestones we have indicated. This contributes mightily to a shared understanding that Catholic colleges and universities are guided by a mission and a purpose that transcends and unites academic disciplines in pursuit of the unity of knowledge and a celebration of the dialogue between faith and reason.

3. NEW PROGRAMS AND/OR STRUCTURES: CATHOLIC STUDIES

The health of any institution is both its ability over time to deepen its mission and to find new and innovative forms to express this mission.[31] As discussed in Chapter One, the enduring principles of the unity of knowledge and the complementarity of faith and reason define the distinctive character of a Catholic university, but the form and structure of the university can change and be expressed in different ways at different times. This dynamic between form and principle has been a *modus operandi* of the Church for over two thousand years. Pope Benedict XVI explained that "[i]n the course of history, this [the Church's apostolic] mission has taken on new forms and employed new strategies according to different places, situations, and historical periods."[32] The Church and its institutions such as the university is *semper reformanda* (ever reforming).[33] Here one recalls the adage Newman expressed: "To live is to change, and to be perfect is to have changed often."[34] We must develop new forms and structures within the university since we are constantly engaging a changing culture. Remaining the same structurally and programmatically will most likely not work for the rapidly changing culture we find ourselves in. Yet, for as liberal and progressive as many faculty members claim to be, they can be very conservative in terms of their resistance to changing structures and programs. We do not change, however, in order to become something else, but rather to remain true to the enduring principles upon which we are founded.

One such change in the last twenty-five years has been the phenomenon of Catholic Studies programs in Catholic universities. The first Catholic Studies program started in the early 1990s at the University of St. Thomas in St. Paul, Minnesota. It serves as an invitation to participate in the integrating power of the Incarnation in both life and thought. It has grown over the years into an enterprise with a diverse array of academic programs, institutes, and projects. It has sparked the founding of over fifty similar Catholic Studies programs and initiatives across the country and around the world. The claims of Catholic Studies are both potent and modest. Its potency comes from its interdisciplinary vision, ecclesial commitment, and collegiate community. Its modesty is in its limits. We will explore both below.

As with any innovation and its impact, it is important to understand both the context of its beginnings and the principles upon which it has gone forward. Catholic Studies did not start off with a carefully worked-out blueprint theorized in advance and meticulously put into play. Like many movements, it progressed under guiding principles rather than under specific bureaucratic structures. It did not, for example, construct an

ideal curriculum or some complete structure of programs, nor did it have great resources. The focus was a
community of scholars and teachers from different disciplines whose commitment was not to a disciplinary
method, but to the principles articulated in Chapter
Two—the unity of knowledge and the complementarity of faith and reason.

Part of the difficulty for some in understanding
Catholic Studies as a movement within Catholic universities is that it appears to signal a loss of identity for
the university as a whole, and it isolates the mission
and identity to a small group of people within the university. However, this often stems from a short-sighted
view of Catholic Studies as well as a misunderstanding
of Catholic universities in the past. First, as we noted
above, it has always been true that only a minority of
faculty at Catholic institutions have systematically
engaged the complex intellectual search for a unity of
knowledge arising out of a Catholic vision of reality.
In the past, this task was largely accomplished by the
religious communities that founded and sustained
these institutions, communities such as the Christian
Brothers, Jesuits, Sisters of Mercy, and other religious
orders whose own communal conversations established a framework and context for the university as a
whole. The decline in numbers and influence of these
religious communities has left a large void within
Catholic universities and it is perhaps inevitable that

the now more voluntary and diverse community of largely lay scholars committed to an ongoing inter-disciplinary reflection on the integrity of Catholic life and thought would continue to be a minority of the faculty as a whole. Therefore, the work of Catholic Studies is not only an academic and intellectual proj-ect, but also an ecclesial and apostolic one.

Second, Catholic Studies, precisely as an interdis-ciplinary project, seeks connections throughout the university, finding ways to concretely foster the unity of knowledge and dialogue between faith and reason. It seeks not just connections within the humanities but also the natural sciences, social sciences and especially the professional schools where an increasing number of students seek their majors. Through faculty semi-nars, interdisciplinary courses, research projects, and conferences, Catholic Studies has created forums that give faculty and students the space and time to explore the connections among disciplines. Most students, for example, who major or minor in Catholic Studies also major in another field like business, engineering, neu-roscience, biology, philosophy, or history. The Catholic Studies major and minor are designed to be interdisci-plinary, to connect with other fields. It is not designed to create its own method and language to be a stand-alone major. With the increasing specialization of dis-ciplines and the career-oriented character of students, without new interdisciplinary projects that seek the unity of knowledge, the default will be fragmentation and careerism.[35]

While Catholic Studies is and has been an indispensable work of renewal, it is also clear that it is, in itself, insufficient to realize the purpose of the Catholic university. It can serve as a catalyst for reflection and renewal in forming a generation of students and can provide forums for sustained reflection on the history and contemporary relevance of Catholic thought and culture for faculty. Catholic Studies, however, cannot replace the larger university-wide task of creating the robust hiring for mission plans and faculty development programs for the university that are articulated in this chapter. This is the responsibility of university trustees, of the president and senior administration and faculty. If Catholicism is to be "perceptibly present and effectively operative" within the Catholic university, it will require a more comprehensive effort than Catholic Studies can provide.[36] Nonetheless, Catholic Studies constitutes one of those creative components on which larger (in this case academic) cultures depend. As such it reminds us of the great tradition of Catholic thought and culture and invites students and faculty to an encounter with those great things that Dante described as the source of awe and wonder on which the soul finally depends.[37]

4. GOVERNANCE: ROLE OF THE TRUSTEES

Finally, and briefly, we turn to the importance of governance in the university. The etymology of the word "govern" is to "steer or navigate." One cannot steer something well if one doesn't know its destination or the "purpose of the trip." To govern then means to steer an institution and to get everyone, and in particular leadership, moving in the right direction. Key to institutional steering for university trustees is the following question: How do we know as trustees whether the mission is alive and well at the university?

Board structure is a significant variable as we consider this question. Historically, boards of directors and trustees have been structured with standing subcommittees that focus attention on important fiduciary duties. In addition to an executive committee, common board committees include an audit and/or finance committee, a leadership succession (or nominating) committee, a capital campaign committee for nonprofits, and a board development and evaluation committee. While the Catholic mission should animate all of these committees, the fact is that mission-related issues can easily get lost in the details and logistics.

What Catholic universities should institutionalize is a "mission oversight committee" of the board whose charge is to pay special attention to the maintenance of

the university's foundational platform in the unity of
knowledge and the complementarity of faith and reason. Appointments to this standing committee should
include board members who have a strong interest and
familiarity with the aspirations and ideals of the Catholic university, especially those trustees who are open
and receptive to a deeper intellectual formation in the
purpose of a Catholic university. Many boards are pop-
ulated by businesspeople who bring to the university
managerial and leadership vision, financial expertise
and resources, and an outside perspective that can pre-
vent the university from succumbing to its own insular
temptations. However, when boards are disconnected
from the deeply intellectual and theological root system articulated in Chapter One, they default to running
the university like a business, which may benefit the
university in the short term, but in the long term will
sever the university from its mission and identity.

One tool that Catholic health care has used to assess
its mission for boards and sponsors is the "Catholic
Identity Matrix" (CIM).[38] Modeled on the assessment
approach from the Baldrige Performance Excellence
Program, the CIM integrates the organization's core
principles with an assessment framework that helps
boards and leaders discern how well it is integrating its
mission with the specific operating policies and practices of the institution. Catholic university boards of
trustees could adapt such a tool to the principles of the

unity of knowledge and complementarity of faith and reason that would help specify in greater detail whether the mission is alive and well at the university.

CONCLUSION

Today, we need trustees, presidents, administrators, and faculty who have the practical wisdom that involves what Cicero described as a "*memory* of the past, *understanding* of the present, and *foresight*_in regard to the future."[39] If leaders of Catholic universities hope to impart wisdom to their students, they must gain a *memory* of the past; specifically, they will need a deep understanding of the principles of Catholic higher education as they have developed over the past two thousand years. When we know on whose shoulders we stand, we can better understand our present role in *passing on the fire* of this tradition, and we can more wisely cultivate the foresight needed to *sustain and develop* Catholic colleges and universities into the future. If we are ignorant of the tradition, we will be hampered in understanding our current circumstances and will be ill-equipped to face the challenges of the future.

There are significant pressures that can undermine the core principles of a Catholic university: the declining financial margins of universities; the significant decline in the humanities both in terms of general requirements and in terms of majors and minors; the increasing specialization of disciplines repressing avenues to explore the unity of knowledge; the increasing secularization marginalizing faith and theology in academic discourse; and the sheer bureaucratic force of the institution losing sight of its deeper commitments. To think that leading Catholic universities is an easy task is naïve and dangerous. Yet, it is precisely from such difficulties that new opportunities arise to renew the Catholic university. Such opportunities are in front of us. We need leaders of vision and virtue especially the virtues of wisdom and courage to guide us forward.

ENDNOTES

1   Kenneth Goodpaster, *Conscience and Corporate Culture* (Malden, Mass.: Wiley-Blackwell, 2007), chapter 6.

2   "Seven S Framework for General Management," Chapter 4 of Richard Tanner, Pascale & Anthony Athos, *The Art of Japanese Management: Applications for American Executives,* (New York: Warner Books, 1981), 122. In this chapter, McKinsey and Company's framework represents one approach to the "syntax" of institutionalization.

3   It has often been suggested that the design and membership of boards of directors and boards of trustees be approached primarily with "diversity" in a "representative" fashion. These are sometimes referred to as "constituency boards." But practical wisdom and experience has shown that such boards are ineffective because they do not have in common

the two things necessary to function in a unified and collaborative manner: clarity about and commitment to the corporate mission.

4 See Melanie M. Morey and Dennis H. Holtschneider, "Leadership and the Age of the Laity: Emerging Patterns in Catholic Higher Education," in *Catholic Higher Education: An Emerging Paradigm for the Twenty-First Century*, ed. Anthony J. Cernera (Fairfield, Conn.: Sacred Heart University Press, 2005), 19.

5 James L. Heft, SM, and Fred P. Pestello, "Hiring Practices in Catholic Colleges and Universities," *Current Issues in Catholic Higher Education* 20 (Fall 1999): 89–97.

6 Don Briel, "Mission and Identity: The Role of Faculty," *Journal of Catholic Higher Education* 31, no. 2 (2012): 169.

7 Pope Francis, Encyclical Letter *Veritatis Gaudium* (January 29, 2018), 4.

8 In 2004, Joseph Ratzinger (later Pope Benedict XVI) wrote "The tree of the Kingdom of God reaches beyond the branches of the visible Church, but that is precisely why it must be a hospitable place in whose branches many guests find solace." This image of a tree fed by the Catholic intellectual tradition that provides a home and a nesting place for guests of many traditions who share in the life of the tree is a helpful way to think of the identity *and* the diversity of a Catholic university. Ratzinger contended that schools face a new challenge, that of "the coming together of religions and cultures in the joint search for truth." This means, he said, on the one hand, "not excluding anyone in the name of their cultural or religious background," and on the other "not stopping at the mere recognition" of this cultural or religious difference. Joseph Ratzinger and Marcello Pera, *Without Roots: The West, Relativism, Christianity, Islam* (New York: Hachette Books, 2004), 122.

9   Regarding faculty sacramental participation, Steve Cortright
     explains that "What is radically Catholic is not a code of mor-
     als nor even a credal statement, but an action: the Passover of
     the Lord. What is proposed for faith is not proposition, but
     event." Cortright speaks of the importance of "sacramental
     identification" as the defining center of a Catholic university.
     When this center is marginalized, the university's ecclesial
     commitment is not far behind. Steve Cortright, "Sacramen-
     tal Identification," Address to 7th International Symposium
     on Catholic Social Thought and Management Education,
     University of Notre Dame, June 11–13, 2008.

10   John Paul II, Apostolic Constitution *Ex corde ecclesiae*
     (August 15, 1990), 9, mentions "the Christian mind" and
     "advancing higher culture."

11   John Paul II, *Ex corde ecclesiae*, Article 4, §2.

12   John Paul II, *Ex corde ecclesiae*, Article 4, §3.

13   On the legal front, a recent ruling by the National Labor
     Relations Board indicates that hiring decisions by faith-
     based institutions of higher education are protected by the
     First Amendment of the U.S. Constitution. 361 NLRB 1404,
     Pacific Lutheran University and Service Employees Inter-
     national Union, Local 925, Case 19-RC-102521 (December
     16, 2014).

14   In *Ex corde ecclesiae,* John Paul II states the following: "In
     order not to endanger the Catholic identity of the Uni-
     versity or Institute of Higher Studies, the number of non-
     Catholic teachers should not be allowed to constitute a
     majority within the Institution, which is and must remain
     Catholic" (II:4.4). Corroborating the mandates of *Ex corde
     ecclesiae*, D. Paul Sullins found that Catholic faculty at
     Catholic universities showed "higher support for Catho-
     lic identity in latent structures of aspiration for improved

Catholic distinctiveness, a desire for more theology or philosophy courses, and longer institutional tenure." D. Paul Sullins, "The Difference Catholic Makes: Catholic Faculty and Catholic Identity," *Journal for the Scientific Study of Religion 43*, no. 1 (2004): 83–101.

15 Kenneth Goodpaster and Michael Naughton in discussion with Fr. Robert Sullivan, December 21, 2019.

16 To place this excerpt in context, here is the full text of the Notre Dame Mission Statement:

"The University of Notre Dame is a Catholic academic community of higher learning, animated from its origins by the Congregation of Holy Cross. The University is dedicated to the pursuit and sharing of truth for its own sake. As a Catholic university, one of its distinctive goals is to provide a forum where, through free inquiry and open discussion, the various lines of Catholic thought may intersect with all the forms of knowledge found in the arts, sciences, professions, and every other area of human scholarship and creativity.

The intellectual interchange essential to a university requires, and is enriched by, the presence and voices of diverse scholars and students. The Catholic identity of the University depends upon, and is nurtured by, the continuing presence of a predominant number of Catholic intellectuals. This ideal has been consistently maintained by the University leadership throughout its history. What the University asks of all its scholars and students, however, is not a particular creedal affiliation, but a respect for the objectives of Notre Dame and a willingness to enter into the conversation that gives it life and character. Therefore, the University insists upon academic freedom that makes open discussion and inquiry possible."

17   It is important to point out that the database of the Office
     for Academic Mission Support is used exclusively to assist
     recruitment and hiring decisions, not for tenure and pro-
     motion decisions.

18   It should be noted that while recruitment and hiring should
     normally be located at the level of the department or school,
     this is not an absolute.

19   Timothy Kirchoff, "Universities Must Fashion, Not Just
     'Find,' Catholic Faculty," *Ethika Politika* (December 1,
     2014): https://ethikapolitika.org/2014/12/01/universities
     -must-fashion-just-find-catholic-faculty/. He writes "But in
     many disciplines, recovering that which has been lost need
     not come at the price of what has been gained. Universi-
     ties must not only hire scholars amenable to their Catholic
     mission, but find ways to invite these scholars to integrate
     Catholic insights into their work and furthermore to see
     this sort of integration as an indispensable part of their
     vocation as academics. If these opportunities for integra-
     tion, though they may be hosted by departments, centers,
     or institutes, are made readily available and it is clear that
     the university as an institution is investing in these efforts,
     we may be surprised to see just how many professors leap
     at the chance to participate more fully in their respective
     universities' Catholic missions."

20   Kirchoff, "Universities Must Fashion, Not Just 'Find,' Cath-
     olic Faculty."

21   Morey and Holtschneider, in their study of Catholic uni-
     versity presidents, express concerns over the lack of lead-
     ership formation related to mission and culture: "[W]ith
     little or no formal preparation, formation, or study, lay
     men and women enter Catholic College and university
     presidencies with a distinct leadership disadvantage. It

would seem that this lack of religious education and formation could have a negative impact on the enterprise of
Catholic higher education. Presidents, however, do not
seem convinced, nor do the institutions they serve." See
Melanie M. Morey and Dennis H. Holtschneider, "Leadership and the Age of the Laity."

22   It is our conviction that retirement provisions in Catholic
universities should include "phased" retirement options
over a two- or three-year period. Otherwise both the
retiree and the university can suffer from the *abruptness* of
retirement departures.

23   Kirchoff, "Universities Must Fashion, Not Just 'Find,'
Catholic Faculty": "Contemporary conversations about
preserving or rebuilding the Catholic identities of prom-
inent American Catholic universities (that, is, those with
research arms, as distinct from smaller liberal arts colleges)
often revolve around the mandate in *Ex corde ecclesiae* to
maintain a majority-Catholic faculty, and therefore the
need for these Catholic universities to find and hire Catholic scholars. This recommendation is fundamentally sound,
but the task is not as simple as it may seem at first: Religious
identification alone cannot predict a scholar's potential
interest in or contribution to the Catholic mission of a university. We might readily point out that not every scholar
who identifies as Catholic will necessarily be substantively
so and might not be invested in the Catholic mission of
the institution. The converse—that a non-Catholic scholar
can be an active and enthusiastic contributor to that mission—might not be equally obvious, but it is nonetheless
true. Those who have had the chance to closely study Catholic thought (and especially Catholic social thought) often
find it to be a useful dialectic for their research as well as a

way of relating more effectively to their Catholic students. These faculty needn't be Catholic themselves to appreciate and communicate the depth and complexity of the Catholic intellectual tradition."

24 Melanie Morey and Dennis Holtschneider, "Study on Campus Links to Religious Sponsors," *Association of Governing Boards of Colleges and Universities* (Washington, D.C., 2000): http://www.collegium.org/node/117. They add: "One of the most significant losses Catholic colleges experience as congregation members disappear is the loss of witness. Therefore, a critical question they face in maintaining their unique cultural identity is how to create witnesses without religious congregations."

25 Morey and Holtschneider, "Study on Campus Links to Religious Sponsors."

26 Bill George, *Authentic Leadership: Rediscovering the Secrets to Creating Lasting Value* (Hoboken, N.J.: John Wiley & Sons, 2003), 75.

27 For versions of the seminar, contact Michael Naughton at mjnaughton@stthomas.edu.

28 "Collegium: A Colloquy on Faith and Intellectual Life." Collegium. https://www.collegium.org/.

29 "Business and Catholic Social Thought: A Primer," a conference collaboration between the University of St. Thomas (Minn.), The Catholic University of America (D.C.) and the University of Notre Dame, http://lumenchristi.org/seminars /1777.

30 Andre Delbecq, "A Leadership Perspective on Catholic Business Education" (Address, 7th International Symposium on Catholic Social Thought and Management Education, University of Notre Dame, June 11–13, 2008). Andre Delbecq, "An Ignatian Faculty Forum," *Explore* 6, no. 2

(Spring 2003): 28–32. See also http://www.ajcunet.edu
/march-2018-connections/2018/2/26/santa-clara-university
-thematic.

31   This section was adapted from speeches given by Don Briel
at the St. Mary's College in Moraga, California, March 3,
2001 and his speech at the University of Mary. Versions of
these speeches can be found in Don Briel, *The University
and the Church*, ed. R. Jared Staudt (Providence, R.I.: Cluny
Media, 2019).

32   Benedict XVI, Apostolic Letter *Ubicumque et semper* (September 21, 2010).

33   Henri de Lubac cautioned how our reforms play out. He
wrote: "I do not believe that structural reforms, about
which there has been much debate for some years, are ever
the main part of a program that must aim at the only true
renewal, spiritual renewal. I even fear that the present-day
inflation of such projects and discussions furnishes an
all-too-convenient alibi to avoid it. The conciliar formula
"Ecclesia semper purificanda" [Church ever purifying]
seems to me as to others much superior to the 'Ecclesia
semper reformanda' which is used so extensively nearly
everywhere." Quoted in Avery Cardinal Dulles, "True and
False Reform," *First Things* (August 2003): https://www
.firstthings.com/article/2003/08/true-and-false-reform.

34   John Henry Newman, *An Essay on the Development of Doctrine* (London: Longmans, Green, and Co., 1909), 41.

35   It is important here to distinguish the work of interdisciplinary and multidisciplinary studies. The task of interdisciplinary studies is to integrate the methods and insights
of a variety of disciplines within a complex but coherent
vision of reality. In contrast, multidisciplinary studies seek
to take into account the autonomous methods and insights

of a variety of disciplinary perspectives while leaving their mutual relations autonomous. The first lends itself to the pursuit of the unity of knowledge and the study of the relations of faith and reason. The latter does not. This is why academic theology, although indispensable in this work, would be insufficient in itself to achieve it. We need to recover the imaginative tradition of the faith, its approach to beauty, the great-souled world of literature, the deep artistic traditions of Catholicism, its understanding of the human person and of the range and the limits of politics. For we share the view of Dawson that "the Christian culture of the past was an organic whole. It was not confined to theology, it expressed itself also in philosophy and in literature, in art and music, society and institutions, and none of these forms of expression can be understood completely unless they are seen in relation to the rest. But under existing conditions this is impossible." Christopher Dawson, "Civilization in Crisis," in *Christianity and European Culture,* ed. Gerald J. Russello (Washington, D.C.: The Catholic University of America Press, 1998), 79.

[36]   "Land O'Lakes Statement on the Nature of the Contemporary Catholic University" (July 23, 1967), section 1.

[37]   Dante Alighieri, *Convivio*, trans. William Walrond Jackson (Oxford: Oxford University Press, 1909), 281.

[38]   Dean Maines, "Self-Assessment and Improvement Process," *Wiley Encyclopedia of Management*, vol. 2, ed. C. L. Cooper (Chichester, UK: John Wiley & Sons Ltd., 2014), 425–428.

[39]   Cicero, *De Inventione* II, 53, quoted by Thomas Aquinas, *Summa Theologiae* (*ST*) I-II, q. 57, a. 6.

EPILOGUE

Examination of Conscience

As argued throughout this essay, Catholic univer-sities need a contemplative outlook. To foster this outlook, we end with an ongoing examination of conscience that can simultaneously foster *humility* in leaders in what they need to acknowledge as well as *boldness* in institutionalizing the purpose of the Cath-olic university.

In an address to the Roman Curia, Pope Francis invited its members to a provocative "examination of conscience." He explained that each person in the Curia who is not nourished with spiritual food "will become a bureaucrat (a formalist, a functionalist, an employee): a shoot that dries up and little by little dies and is thrown away."[1] This is a danger for *all* leaders—to become mere bureaucrats—people who lose sight of the deeper pur-poses of their institutions and manage them through mechanical procedures and/or superficial slogans or

branding. To institutionalize the purpose of an organization is to act with a significant intention and
direction, rather than leaving matters to chance or to
external forces. Conscience is our primary check on
the institutional teleopathy that we have described in
Chapter Three. The ethical discipline known as "the
examination of conscience" (or in Ignatian spirituality "The Examen") describes a technique not only for
personal, but also for institutional self-assessment and
improvement.[2] The task of leading Catholic universities
requires the virtue of practical wisdom, necessitating
great effort, complex assessment, and difficult decisions. But at the heart of this practical wisdom will be
a contemplative mind and heart that can receive what
the Lord is calling us to do. So we end our reflection
with the following questions that may help in formu-
lating such an examination for faculty, senior leaders
and trustees:

- Do I, and does this college or university, *understand* the foundational role played by the basic
  principles of the Catholic intellectual tradition,
  most notably the unity of knowledge and the
  ultimate complementarity of faith and reason? If
  not, are there steps that can be taken to remedy
  this state of affairs?
- Do I appreciate the *institutional trust* that has
  been placed in me as a leader in my college or
  university community to protect and enhance its

Catholic mission and identity in the spirit of *Ex corde ecclesiae*?

- Does the leadership of this college or university appreciate the difference between *institutional mission and identity* and *institutional diversity*, that is, the difference between remaining true to its mission and identity while welcoming faculty, staff, and students from every corner of the human community who seek to participate in furthering that mission and identity?

- Are there teleopathic tendencies in how we articulate and nurture the purpose of this college or university? What forms of *fixation* are we prone to? What kinds of *rationalization* do we default to? What goods or principles are we liable to *detach from*? For example, does the college/university foster true diversity of thought in its classrooms, student activities, and outside speaker programs, avoiding ideological or political biases and partisanship?

- Are there institutional policies or practices at this college or university that tend to *erode* its distinctive mission and identity? Do we appreciate how such policies or practices came about and how best to reform or eliminate them? For example, are there policies regarding speech or expression by students that might make some feel reluctant to share their ideas in dialogue (liberal or conservative)?

- What are the gaps between the *aspirational* language articulated in our mission statement and the language of *practice* or *"values-in-action"* driven by the incentives, rewards, hiring and promotion systems of the organization? Are they fully aligned? Or is there institutional "hypocrisy" (a disconnect between institutional "talk" and "walk")? Does the college/university regularly invite discussion of such "gaps" among members of the academic community?
- If we *understand* the pillars of the Catholic university, how do we institutionalize them?
  - In *recruitment* and *hiring*? In the appointment of search committees? In the choice of search firms?
  - In *strategic* planning, board *structure*, and measurement *systems,* including criteria for promotion and tenure among faculty?
  - In *curricular design*, including the central role of theology and philosophy?
  - In faculty and leadership *formation*? "Milestone retreats"?
  - In new governance structures and academic programs?
- Finally, do I as a leader accept the fullness of the contemplative and more deep-rooted purpose of the university, a vision of the world that *receives* reality rather than *constructs* it? Do I

embrace a contemplative outlook that listens "to the being of things," captured by wonder, imagination, prayer and praise?

ENDNOTES

1   Pope Francis, *Address to Roman Curia*, December 23, 2014.
2   For an institutional examination of conscience, see the Dicastery for Promoting Integral Human Development, *Vocation of the Business Leader* (2018): https://www.stthomas .edu/media/catholicstudies/center/ryan/publications /publicationpdfs/vocationofthebusinessleaderpdf/Final TextTheVocationoftheBusinessLeader.pdf.

RECOMMENDED READING

Briel, Don, Kenneth Goodpaster, and Michael Naughton. "Our Reason for Being: Restoring the Pillars of Catholic Education." *America Magazine* (February 1, 2016), https://www.americamagazine.org/issue/our-reason-being.

Briel, Don. "Mission and Identity: The Role of Faculty." *Journal of Catholic Higher Education* 31, no. 2 (2012): 169–179.

———. *University and the Church.* Edited by R. Jared Staudt. Providence, R.I.: Cluny Media, 2019.

Benedict XVI. *Apostolic Journey to München, Altötting and Regensburg: Meeting with the Representatives of Science in the Aula Magna of the University of Regensburg.* September 12, 2006. This is also sometimes cited as "Three Stages in the Program of De-Hellenization" (Papal Address at University of Regensburg).

———. *Meeting with Representatives from the World of Culture.* Address. September 12, 2008.

———. *Caritas in Veritate.* Encyclical Letter. June 29, 2009.

Brooks, David. "The Organization Kid." *The Atlantic Monthly* (April 2001): 40–54.

Buckley, Michael, SJ. "The Catholic University and Its Inherent Promise." *America,* 168, no. 19 (May 29, 1993): 14, http://www.bc.edu/content/dam/files/offices/mission/pdf1/cu24.pdf.

———. *The Catholic University as Promise and Project.* Washington, D.C.: Georgetown University Press, 1998.

Burtchaell, James. *The Dying of the Light: The Disengagement of Colleges and Universities from Their Christian Churches.* Grand Rapids, Mich.: Eerdmans, 1998.

Cavadini, John C. "Open Letter to the University Community." *The Observer* (April 19, 2006, updated September 12, 2012). https://ndsmcobserver.com/2006/04/open-letter-to-the-university-community/.

Daly, Lawrie J., SJ. *The Medieval University 1200–1400*. New York: Sheed and Ward, 1961.

Dawson, Christopher. *The Crisis of Western Education*. Washington, D.C.: The Catholic University of America Press, 1961.

Delbecq, Andre. "An Ignatian Faculty Forum." *Explore* 6, no. 2 (Spring 2003): 28–32. See also http://www.ajcunet.edu/march-2018-connections/2018/2/26/santa-clara-university-thematic.

Francis. *Veritatis Gaudium*. Apostolic Constitution. January 29, 2018.

George, Francis, OMI. "Universities that are Truly Catholic and Truly Academic." Inaugural Convocation of President and Faculty Members of Chicago Area Catholic Colleges and Universities. September 22, 1998. http://www3.nd.edu/~afreddos/papers/george2.htm.

Giussani, Luigi. *The Risk of Education*. Translated by Mariangela Sullivan. Montreal: McGill-Queen's University Press, 2019.

Goodpaster, Kenneth. *Conscience and Corporate Culture*. Malden, Mass.: Wiley-Blackwell, 2007.

Habiger Institute for Catholic Leadership. *The Heart of Culture: A Brief History of Western Education*. Providence, R.I.: Cluny Media, 2020.

Heclo, Hugh. *On Thinking Institutionally*. Boulder, Colo.: Paradigm Publishers, 2008.

Heft, James L., SM, and Fred P. Pestello. "Hiring Practices in Catholic Colleges and Universities." *Current Issues in Catholic Higher Education* 20 (Fall 1999): 89–97.

John Paul II. *Ex Corde Ecclesiae*. Apostolic Constitution. August 15, 1990.

———. *Centesimus Annus.* Encyclical Letter. May 1, 1991.

———. *Fides et Ratio.* Encyclical Letter. September 14, 1998.

Kerr, Clark. *The Uses of the University.* Cambridge, Mass./London, UK: Harvard University Press, 2001.

Leclercq, Jean, OSB. *The Love of Learning and the Desire for God.* New York: Fordham University Press, 1961.

Lewis, C. S. *The Abolition of Man.* New York: HarperCollins Publishers, 2000, originally published 1944.

———. "First and Second Things." In *C.S. Lewis First and Second Things,* edited by Walter Hooper. Glasgow: Collins Fount Paperbacks, 1985.

Lewis, Harry R. *Education without a Soul: How a Great University Forgot Education.* New York: Public Affairs, 2006.

MacIntyre, Alasdair. "Dangers, Hopes, Choices." In *Higher Learning & Catholic Traditions,* edited by R. E. Sullivan, 1–21. Notre Dame, Ind.: University of Notre Dame Press, 2001.

———. "The Very Idea of a University: Aristotle, Newman and Us." *New Blackfriars* 91, no. 1031 (2010): 4–19. First published in *British Journal of Education Studies* 57, no. 4 (December 2009): 347–362.

Maritain, Jacques. *Education at the Crossroads.* New Haven, Conn.: Yale University Press, 1943.

Marrou, H. I. *A History of Education in Antiquity.* Madison, Wisc.: The University of Wisconsin Press, 1956.

Morey, Melanie M. and Dennis H. Holtschneider. "Leadership and the Age of the Laity: Emerging Patterns in Catholic Higher Education." In *Catholic Higher Education: An Emerging Paradigm for the Twenty-First Century,* edited by A. J. Cernera, 3–27. Fairfield, Conn.: Sacred Heart University Press, 2005.

Newman, John Henry. *The Idea of a University.* Notre Dame, Ind.: University of Notre Dame Press, 1987. First published in 1852.

———. "Rise and Progress of Universities." In *Historical Sketches Vol. III*, 1–251. London: Longman's Green and Co., 1924.

Paul VI. *Evangelii Nuntiandi*. Apostolic Exhortation. December 8, 1975.

Pieper, Josef. *Leisure: The Basis of Culture*. South Bend, Ind.: St. Augustine's Press, 1998.

Shirmpton, Paul. *The 'Making of Men': The Idea and Reality of Newman's University in Oxford and Dublin*. London: Gracewing, 2014.

Sullins, D. Paul. "The Difference Catholic Makes: Catholic Faculty and Catholic Identity." *Journal for the Scientific Study of Religion* 43, no. 1 (2004): 83–101.

Sommerville, C. John. *The Decline of the Secular University*. Oxford: Oxford University Press, 2006.

Topping, Ryan, ed. *Renewing the Mind: A Reader in the Philosophy of Catholic Education*. Washington, D.C.: The Catholic University of America Press, 2015.

Twenge, Jean M. *iGen: Why Today's Super-Connected Kids Are Growing Up Less Rebellious, More Tolerant, Less Happy—and Completely Unprepared for Adulthood—and What That Means for the Rest of Us*. New York: Atria Paperback, 2017.

Weil, Simone. *The Need for Roots: Prelude to a Declaration of Duties towards Mankind*. London: Routledge Classics, 2002.

INDEX

AUTHORS' BIOGRAPHIES

Don Briel completed his theological studies at the University of Strasbourg. He wrote his dissertation on Newman under the direction of Maurice Nedoncelle. In 1981, he began teaching at the University of St. Thomas, where he later chaired the department of theology, founded the program in Catholic Studies, and became the Koch chair and director of the Center for Catholic Studies. He has written and lectured widely on Catholic higher education. He served as the general editor of *The Works of Christopher Dawson* (Catholic University of America Press). He also served on a number of national advisory boards and the board of trustees of the American Academy for Liberal Education. In September of 2014 he was appointed the Newman Chair in the Liberal Arts at the University of Mary and also served as a fellow at the Lumen Christi Institute in Chicago. Dr. Briel died on February 15, 2018.

Kenneth E. Goodpaster earned his AB in mathematics from the University of Notre Dame and his AM and PhD in philosophy from the University of Michigan. Goodpaster taught graduate and undergraduate philosophy at the University of Notre Dame throughout the 1970s before joining the Harvard Business School faculty in 1980, where he developed the ethics curriculum. In 1990 Goodpaster left Harvard to accept the David and Barbara Koch Endowed Chair in Business Ethics at the University of St. Thomas. At St. Thomas, he taught in the full-time and part-time MBA programs. His publications include *Conscience and Corporate Culture* (Wiley-Blackwell, 2007) and *Policies and Persons: A Casebook in Business Ethics* (McGraw-Hill, 2006). He also contributed to the *Vocation of the Business Leader*, issued by the Dicastery for Promoting Integral Human Development (2012). Most recently Goodpaster served as executive editor of a much-anticipated history, *Corporate Responsibility: The American Experience* (Cambridge University Press, 2012) which received the 2014 Academy of Management Best Book Award. He was recently named to *Ethisphere Magazine*'s annual list of the *100 Most Influential People in Business Ethics.* Goodpaster is now professor emeritus in the Opus College of Business.

Michael J. Naughton has been a teacher for over 35 years. He is the director of the Center for Catholic Studies at the University of St. Thomas in St. Paul, Minnesota, and holder of the Koch Chair in Catholic Studies where he is a full professor in the department of Catholic Studies. He also taught in the Opus College of Business for twenty years. He is the co-author and co-editor of eleven books and over sixty articles. He helped coordinate and write the *Vocation of the Business Leader* issued by the Vatican's Dicastery for Promoting Integral Human Development, which has been translated into fifteen languages. Naughton serves as board chair for Reell Precision Manufacturing, a global producer of innovative torque solutions for transportation, consumer electronics, medical, and office automation products. He is also a trustee at the University of Mary. He received his PhD in theology from Marquette University (1991) and an MBA from the University of St. Thomas (1995). He is married with five children.

Printed in the USA
CPSIA information can be obtained
at www.ICGtesting.com
LVHW051739131023
760943LV00044BA/651

9 780813 233802